Museums of Chicago

Westholme Museum Guides

Museums of Atlanta
Museums of Boston
Museums of Chicago
Museums of Los Angeles
Museums of New York City
Museums of Philadelphia
Museums of San Francisco

Visiting museums is one of the best ways to get to know a city.
Westholme Museum Guides, designed for both residents and visitors,
are the first-ever uniform compilations of permanent collections open to
the public in America's major cities. Each city has its own unique group
of museums, some famous, others practically unknown, but all of them
are important parts of our nation's cultural life.

Museums of Chicago

A Guide for Residents and Visitors

Susan I. Phillips

WESTHOLME
Yardley

Acknowledgments
I would like to thank the dedicated museum staff and volunteers who provided information for this book, John Hubbard for his cover design, and Christine Liddie for her copyediting. I am grateful to Bruce Franklin for the opportunity to write this book, to Laura Waldron for her lovely example, and to my husband, Mike, for his enthusiasm and support.

Published by Westholme Publishing, LLC, Eight Harvey Avenue, Yardley, Pennsylvania 19067.

Maps by Joseph John Clark

10 9 8 7 6 5 4 3 2 1
First Printing

ISBN 1-59416-010-4

www.westholmepublishing.com

Printed in the United States of America on acid-free paper.

For my mother

Sylvia I. Wells

Contents

Introduction

In 1673 French trader Louis Joliet and Jesuit missionary Jacques Marquette journeyed up the Illinois and Chicago Rivers to reach the southwestern shore of Lake Michigan, becoming the first Europeans to explore the area known as "Checagou," which is often translated as "wild garlic place," but whose precise meaning or even language of origin are not known. Abundant with beaver, bear, otter, black fox, and marten, Chicago was soon established as a major crossroads in the lucrative fur trade. Jean Baptiste Point DuSable, a successful Afro-French fur trader, merchant, and farmer, was Chicago's first permanent non-native resident. Settling in 1788 with his Potawatomi wife, Catherine, DuSable built a large home and trading post on the north banks of the Chicago River not far from the lake's shore. It is fitting that the museum of African American history in Chicago is named in his honor.

With the Greenville Treaty of 1795, natives ceded their land at the mouth of the river to the American government, which led to the establishment of Fort Dearborn, a frontier outpost housing American soldiers and their families. By 1800, the surrounding small community of Native Americans, settlers, and British and French traders became known as Chicago.

In 1833 still little more than a rugged outpost, Chicago was incorporated as a city with a population of 350. A few years later work began on the Illinois and Michigan Canal that created a link for large ships to be able to travel from Lake Michigan and the Chicago River to the Mississippi. The canal transformed Chicago from a frontier city to a thriving industrial metropolis. With its completion in 1848, businessmen flocked from the east coast to Chicago, the new center of Midwestern trade. Corn and lumber shipments increased dramatically, and real estate values rose at an unprecedented rate. Milled lumber built houses, stores, warehouses, sidewalks, bridges, and wharves. Railroads moved even more goods and people, and the population grew to 110,000 by the eve of the Civil War. It was during the construction of the canal that the first major wave of immigrants, Irish laborers, came to Chicago. They were soon followed by successive waves of immigrants, mostly from northern and western Europe. In 1860 European immigrants made up half of Chicago's population. The Irish American Heritage Center and the Swedish American Museum include exhibits dedicated to these early immigrant groups.

In October 1871 the most important event in the history of the city occurred. Whether intentionally or accidentally set, a great fire swept uncontrollably through the heart of Chicago. With the city being built almost entirely of wood, the conflagration burned a swath through the central business district four miles long and a mile wide. Finally extinguished by rain, the Great Fire claimed over 300 lives and left 100,000 homeless. Financial losses totaled more than 250 million dollars. It remains the worst fire in American urban history. Only the stone water tower survived standing as a guidepost for those looking for the remains of their homes and businesses. The water tower and its adjacent pumping station have been preserved and are a distinctive feature of Chicago's downtown.

In typical Chicago fashion, the city rose with confidence and determination from the disaster. The following years were times of unencumbered economic expansion. Civic and business leaders organized support and gave fortunes toward the creation of institutions promoting the arts, sciences, and letters, such as the Chicago Symphony Orchestra and the Newberry Library. At the same time, however, great social inequities developed as barons of industry grew rich at the expense of poorly paid workers spending long hours in scandalously unsafe conditions. The Haymarket riot of 1886 and Pullman strike of 1894 demonstrated the magnitude of a conflict that gave birth to the first labor unions. The Pullman Historic District and the Labor History Museum of the Illinois Labor History Society are devoted to the history of labor and business in Chicago and preserve some of the artifacts and documents from those difficult years.

A second major wave of immigration occurred between 1880 and 1920, when 2.5 million immigrants came to Chicago, mostly from southern and eastern Europe. These included Poles, Italians, Greeks, Bohemians, and Russian Jews. Many immigrants found work in the stockyards, while others found work in construction. Immigrants provided services in their own enclave communities, where ethnic groups clung together for support, maintaining their own schools and churches. While most immigrants did not want to lose their ethnic identities, people from different backgrounds shared many common experiences in their struggle to succeed in a new land. Organizations such as Jane Addams Hull House, part of which has been preserved as a museum, brought groups together with social services and led the way toward progressive reform of urban poverty.

By 1890, with a population of now over a million, Chicago surpassed Philadelphia's standing as the nation's second largest city. Named the Windy City in honor of the politicians and businessmen who boasted of the city's achievements, Chicago sought to shake its reputation as a provincial city by placing itself in the competition to host the 1893 World's Fair. Congress voted to give the World's Columbian Exposition to Chicago, and the city responded in remarkable fashion. A team of the nation's most esteemed architects and craftsmen designed the fair's 200 buildings and public attractions, such as parks, lagoons, moving sidewalks. Dubbed the White City for its brilliantly white neoclassical steel and plaster exhibition halls, the fair featured the world's first Ferris Wheel and exhibits from seventy-two nations, which included displays of machinery, transportation, forestry, agriculture, anthropology, and the arts. Sensational exhibits included an 11-ton block of cheese, a 1,500-pound chocolate Venus de Milo, and Buffalo Bill Cody's Wild West Show. In six months, 27 million guests from all over the world visited the fair and left believing Chicago to be one of the world's greatest cities. Today, the only remaining building from the World's Fair is the Museum of Science and Industry in Frederick Law Olmsted–designed Jackson Park.

Sixteen years after the fair, an ambitious, forward-thinking design, the "Plan of Chicago" called for a system of roadways that connected the Chicago city center to its outlying suburbs within a 60-mile radius as well as the creation of a lakefront park stretching 20 miles along Lake Michigan. Much of the plan was adopted and has given Chicago its broad layout, with spacious Grant Park, the Navy Pier, and the city's wide, scenic roadway, Lake Shore Drive. All of these are part of the experience when visiting Chicago's museums.

The Chicago area continued to expand throughout the twentieth century, with the city's suburbs witnessing rapid growth. Oak Park earned an international reputation through the work of Frank Lloyd Wright, who established a studio in that suburb and designed and built many of its innovative homes.

The city of Chicago is a place where opportunity abounds, where innovation and hard work are rewarded, and where both residents and visitors can enjoy many unique and important attractions, including museums, in one of the nation's most distinctive urban environments.

Chicago Museums

The history and character of Chicago can be told in its many museums. The oldest ones were founded by civic groups and benefactors who saw the need to bring culture and refinement to the rugged frontier town. Among these are the Chicago Academy of Sciences, now known as the Peggy Notebaert Nature Museum, founded in 1857 to preserve the native plants and animals that were rapidly disappearing beneath farms and towns; the Chicago Historical Society, that began to collect and exhibit Lincolniana and other important civic and political materials in 1861; the internationally renowned Art Institute of Chicago, which began in 1866 as the Chicago Academy of Design; and the Newberry Library, named after its benefactor who willed his estate in the 1850s for its establishment.

Chicago Museums range from the colossal Museum of Science and Industry, which houses one of only five remaining U-boats of World War II, along with a passenger jet and collections of train cars and automobiles, to the tiny Labor History Museum, with a concentrated collection of photographs and memorabilia. Museums, such as the Field Museum and DuSable Museum of African-American History, are housed in grand neoclassical buildings surrounded by public parks. Others are located in the heart of neighborhoods with strong ethnic identities. Prestigious universities with fine art museums such as the University of Chicago's Smart Museum, Loyola's Martin D'Arcy Museum of Art, and Northwestern's Mary and Lee Block Museum of Art invite the public to their campuses to enjoy the collections. The city's Harold Washington Library Center, and numerous other private libraries and archives, host permanent and rotating exhibits highlighting their special collections. Historical societies uphold the heritage of communities and organizations by displaying artifacts that testify to the sacrifice and determination of founding generations.

The city's museums are continually updating and expanding. The Museum of Broadcast Communications, which features exhibits on radio and television history, will reopen in a new building on the Near North Side in 2006. The Chicago Historical Society will present reconfigured galleries in 2006, while at the Field Museum a new 24,000-square-foot prehistory exhibit, Evolving Planet, will open in 2006, and in 2007, the museum will unveil a major new exhibit on the Ancient Americas.

The Museum Campus

Some of the greatest museums in the country are located in and near downtown, and many are within walking distance of one another. A mile southeast of downtown, a beautiful view of the city can be admired from the Museum Campus, where the dramatic Chicago skyline silhouettes the north, and Lake Michigan extends east into the horizon. The Field Museum and Adler Planetarium are linked by terraced walkways and gardens, a bike path, and Burnham Harbor. Attractions on the grounds of the Field Museum include a life-size cast of a Brachiosaurus dinosaur, a 55-foot tall totem pole from the Pacific Northwest, and a stone replica of an Olmec Head presented to the city by the State of Veracruz, Mexico. Commemorative public sculpture lines Solidarity Drive to the Adler, where a giant sundial designed by sculptor Henry Moore greets visitors. The world-famous Shedd Aquarium and Soldier Field stadium are also located on the campus, which offers underground parking and restaurants at each venue. On weekends and throughout the summer, free trolleys shuttle visitors downtown and to historic neighborhoods nearby.

The Loop

The Loop refers to the central business district south of the Chicago River where elevated and subway trains traveling from downtown to the outlying neighborhoods turn around. The Art Institute of Chicago is located on Michigan Avenue in the heart of the Loop, in a Beaux Arts building built in conjunction with the Worlds Columbian Exposition of 1893. Across the street is the Chicago Symphony Orchestra Hall, and to the north is the twenty-first century's Millennium Park with gardens, walkways, and monumental interactive sculpture by international contemporary artists Jaume Plensa and Anish Kapoor. A dynamic band shell designed by Frank Gehry and formed with ribbonous steel connects to a snaking bridge across Lake Shore Drive to Grant Park. An impressive collection of public sculpture is sprinkled throughout the Loop, including monumental works by Pablo Picasso, Alexander Calder, Juan Miro, and Marc Chagall. All are located within six square blocks of each other.

North of the Loop

North of the Loop, Navy Pier hosts the Chicago Children's Museum and the Smith Museum of Stained Glass. On Michigan Avenue, the Chicago Tribune skyscraper imbedded with fragments from famous architectural sites from around the world can be admired from the sidewalk. A little further north, the Museum of Contemporary Art presents 45,000 square feet of groundbreaking exhibits by international artists. Nearby, the historical Water Tower and pumping station, two of the only surviving downtown buildings of the Great Fire, offer visitors exhibitions of work by Chicago artists and a tourist information center. Further north on the Gold Coast is the unique International Museum of Surgical Science, housed in a grand 1917 mansion.

Near North Side

The Newberry Library, one of the nation's leading independent research institutions offers fascinating rotating exhibits of special interest to bibliophiles. In Lincoln Park, within walking distance of the zoo, are the Chicago Historical Society and Peggy Notebaert Nature Museum, two of the oldest and most venerable institutions in the city. The Elks Veteran's War Memorial honors its fallen members in a classical domed building furnished with allegorical murals.

South of the Loop

South of the Loop, the galleries of the Museum of Contemporary Photography are located in Columbia College

country, Prairie School designs exist throughout Chicago and its suburbs. Most remain private residences, but the Unity Temple, where Wright was a congregant, represents the style's expansion from private to public spaces.

Cultural Museums

The great cultural diversity of Chicago is represented with pride by organizations that preserve their heritage and chronicle their journey to new lives in the city. With art, artifacts, libraries, and archives, many have established museums in the very neighborhoods where their ancestors settled. Early immigrant groups are represented by modest, newly organized collections at the Irish American Heritage Center and the Chinese American Museum of Chicago. Andersonville's well-established Swedish American Museum, on the north side of the city, recreates the immigration experience for children who are offered an imaginary ride to America in a replicated ocean liner. The Polish Museum of America, housed in the National Headquarters of the Polish Roman Catholic Union of America, represents the second major wave of immigrants, along with the National Ukrainian Museum of Chicago and Balzekas Museum of Lithuanian Culture. The Mexican Fine Arts Center, the largest Mexican cultural institution in the country, is located in Pilsen, a dense and colorful Hispanic neighborhood, where many outdoor murals combine pre-Columbian motifs with contemporary concerns. Hyde Park's DuSable Museum of African American History, named after the black man who was Chicago's first permanent settler, represents the experience of African Americans from slavery through the Civil Rights movement. Chicago's first black community was established in 1840 by fugitive slaves and freed men. During the Great Migration, between 1916 and 1960,

Chicago attracted more than half a million African Americans who left southern states to contribute to Chicago's Black Renaissance in the mid-century. The DuSable chronicles these achievements as well.

Suburbs

Chicago's metropolis stretches past the city limits to municipalities in six surrounding counties. Evanston, the cosmopolitan Chicago suburb directly north of the city, boasts three wonderful museums, the Mary and Leigh Block Museum of Art on the Northwestern University campus, the Charles Gates Dawes House Museum nearby, and the Mitchell Museum of the American Indian of Kendall College. Besides the Frank Lloyd Wright Home and Studio, Oak Park, 10 miles west of city center, also offers the Pleasant Home House Museum and the restored Ernest Hemingway Birth Home and Ernest Hemingway Museum.

The Elmhurst Art Museum, built around one of only three homes designed by Mies van der Rohe, and the Lizzadro Museum of Lapidary Arts are both located in Elmhurst's Wilder Park, 15 miles west of the city. Cantigny Park, the estate of Chicago Tribune publisher Colonel Robert R. McCormick, is located in Wheaton 30 miles west of Chicago. The park features a house museum, military museum and archive, military tank display, and lavish gardens. Just south of Wheaton, in Naperville, Naper Settlement is a historic recreation of a nineteenth century agricultural village. Nathan Manilow Sculpture Park at Governor's State University, in University Park, is one of the nation's largest outdoor art collections. All are worth an hour's trip by car from Chicago. Visitors should consult the Web sites for directions and call ahead to check seasonal hours.

For the purposes of this book, a museum is defined as an institution or organization with a permanent collection of objects that is open to the public. The collection may be on permanent exhibit or displayed on a rotating basis in conjunction with temporary exhibits. Museums listed in this book are mostly located within the city limits. While many Chicago suburbs have active historical societies with displays, and community colleges have their own specialized museums with cultural or scientific programming, only a few have been included in this book. Other important destinations that are not included in this book are the easily accessed Lincoln Park Zoo and Conservatory, Brookfield Zoo, Garfield Park Conservatory, and the world-famous John G. Shedd Aquarium on the Museum Campus. The fabulous Renaissance Society, Hyde Park Art Center, and other fine and historic art galleries that show only rotating exhibits are not included. But these will complement any visit to Chicago's museums or warrant trips in themselves.

Using *Museums of Chicago*

The 70 museums in this guide are listed in alphabetical order by the primary name of the museum or collection. Each entry provides the address, phone number, and Web site for the museum as well as when it is open and what the admission fees are. Since that information can change, it's important to confirm before you go, especially with smaller museums dependent on volunteer help. Calling ahead will inform you about special events and programs, temporary exhibits, and any exhibition that may require additional ticketing. Many museums do not charge an admission fee, but donations are always welcome even when one is not suggested.

Each entry also features symbols to provide a quick reference to tell you if the museum has exhibits for children, if it's best to provide your own transportation, or if you must call ahead before visiting. A key to all of theses symbols is at the end of this section.

Museums are indicated on the maps by page number, making it easy to find which museums are near each other. Many are in or within walking distance of the Loop (downtown business district) or are easily accessed by bus, train, or free trolleys in the summer. Other museums that dot the city and suburbs do require a car. Calling a museum or consulting with an RTA agent will help you find public transportation or the best driving route to your destination.

Following the last museum entry is a section listing museums by different categories, such as the best museums to see on a short trip, those most interesting to teenagers, and the major museums for art, history, or science. These are designed to give guidance in planning your visit.

Further Reading and Resources

Bach, Ira J., and Mary Lackritz Gray. *A Guide to Chicago's Public Sculpture*. University of Chicago Press, 1983

Grossman, James R., Durkin Keating, and Janice L. Reiff, eds. *The Encyclopedia of Chicago*. University of Chicago Press, 2004

Larson, Erik. *The Devil in the White City*. Random House, 2003

Spinney, Robert G. *City of Big Shoulders: A History of Chicago*. Northern Illinois University Press, 2000

Visitor Information

The Chicago Office of Tourism

877-CHICAGO

(312) 744-8599 for the hearing impaired

www.877chicago.com

The office of tourism provides an official travel kit and the toll-free number for responses to visitor inquiries about exhibits, events, accommodations, and sightseeing. The hotline is staffed 24 hours a day, 365 days a year.

Chicago Cultural Center and Visitor Center

78 East Washington Street at Michigan

(312) 744-2400

Open: M-F, 10:00 AM–6:00 PM; Sa, 10:00 AM–5:00 PM; Su, 11:00 AM–5:00 PM; Closed Thanksgiving and Christmas Days

Conveniently located for those visiting the Loop, the Visitor Center is housed on the first floor of the Chicago Cultural Center. Visitor information representatives distribute free publications, maps, and performance schedules. The Cultural Center offers free art exhibitions, modern dance performances, and concerts. Restrooms and a restaurant are located in the center, and underground parking is available in the Grant Park North Garage at Washington and Michigan Avenue.

Chicago's Historic Water Tower Visitor Center

163 East Pearson Avenue

Open every day from 7:30 AM–7:00 PM; Closed Thanksgiving and Christmas Days

The most popular shopping district in Chicago is on the Magnificent Mile, where the center is located on ground level of the historic Water Works building. The center offers information about museums, tourist activities, and events. Restrooms and light snacks are available. Parking is provided for a fee in the Water Tower Place shopping complex, accessed on Chestnut Street.

Chicago Architecture Foundation

Santa Fe Building

224 South Michigan Avenue

Chicago, Illinois 60605

312-922-3432

www.architecture.org

Open every day, 9:30 AM–5:00 PM

Historic and modern skyscraper walking tours and a world-renowned architecture river cruise are the main attractions. In all, 85 different tours by boat, bus, bike, and on foot are offered.

Chicago African American History

www.soulofamerica.com

This Web site offers a history of African American Chicago from 1790 to present and gives information on tours focusing on the south side of Chicago and African American heritage in Chicago.

Chicago Public Library

All Branches

312-747-4300

www.chipublib.org

For residents of Chicago, a limited number of museum passports are available for check-out with a library card. The passport, which can be kept for one week, admits one family to one of several major museums in the city. Call for branch locations and availability.

Regional Transportation

As noted, many museums in the book are accessible on foot from the Loop. The Museum Campus is located a mile and a half southeast of the Loop, and when the weather is good, it's a pleasant walk from the Loop through Grant Park or along the lakefront. On weekends and all summer long, free trolleys pick passengers up downtown, at Navy Pier and Lincoln Park and deliver them to the Museum Campus, Prairie Avenue Historic District, Pilsen, and Chinatown. The Chicago Regional Transit Authority is one of the best transit systems in the country serving almost 2,000,000 daily. All "L" (elevated) and subway trains circle the Loop en route to outlying neighborhoods. METRA trains travel to and from the suburbs. Call for information about Regional Transportation station locations and ticketing.

RTA Customer Service Center

175 West Jackson Boulevard

Suite 250

Chicago, Illinois 60605

312-836-7000

www.rtachicago.com

Maps and schedules for all regional rail, subway, and bus lines are available in printable form from the RTA Web site. Agents are also available for schedule information by phone daily, 4:45 AM–1:00 AM. The service center is open to the public M–F, 8:30 AM–5:00 PM.

Maps

Each museum in this book is marked on the following maps by its page number. These maps are designed to show the reader the general proximity of the museums to one another.

Museums of Chicago

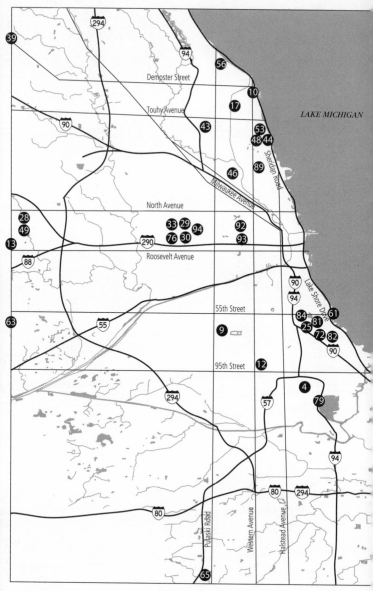

Map No. 1. Museums in greater Chicago. (Each number is museum's book page.)

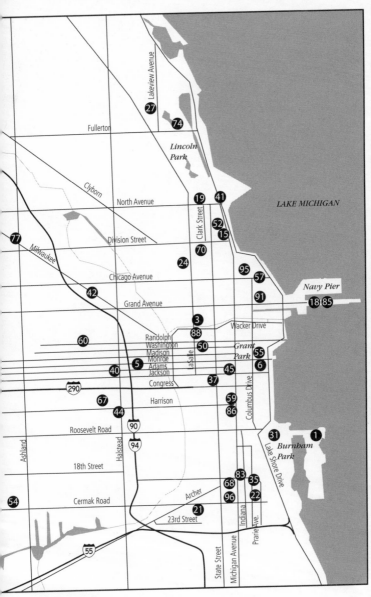

Map No. 2. Museums in and around downtown Chicago.

Visual Codes

Architecturally significant

Best to provide own transportation

Exhibits suitable for children

Food on premises

Must call ahead

Notable art

Notable grounds or garden

Science oriented

Site of historic event

Adler Planetarium and Astronomy Museum

1300 S. Lake Shore Drive
312-922-7827
www.adlerplanetarium.org

Open: M–F, 9:30 AM–4:30 PM; Sa & Su, 9:00 AM–4:30 PM; First Friday of every month, 9:30 AM–10:00 PM
Admission: Adults, $13; Seniors, $12; Children 4–17, $11

As the Western Hemisphere's first planetarium, Adler opened its doors to the public in 1930. From its museum campus location at the end of a peninsula on Burnham Harbor, visitors can enjoy dramatic views of Lake Michigan and the Chicago skyline. A functional 13-foot bronze sundial by sculptor Henry Moore is displayed near the museum's entrance. With more than 35,000 square feet of exhibits, the Adler Planetarium provides an opportunity to learn about the universe through lively displays and interactive adventures.

"Gateway to the Universe" introduces visitors to the realms of space and invites them to experience the feeling of walking in infinite space. Cyberspace is explored through "vision stations," which provide virtual reality experiences of the universe, and 3-D tours of the Milky Way are offered. Visitors learn that many worlds exist in our solar system, and they are invited to design their own at computer stations. Exhibits demonstrate that throughout history humans have sought to understand their place in the universe through observing the sky. Astronomical instruments used by medieval European and Middle Eastern scientists to illustrate concepts of the universe are displayed, including astrolabes, armillary spheres, and sundials. American space exploration is brought to life through a series of original NASA rocket models.

This is the only museum in the world with two full-size planetarium theaters, and visitors can experience the virtual reality environment of the Star Rider Theater or explore the night sky projected on the dome of the historic Zeiss Planetarium Theater. The price of admission includes entrance to one of the two theater showings.

Highlights:
In the fun and interactive "Stranded in an Alien Lab," visitors are invited to imagine their rocket has crash-landed on a strange rocky planet where they discover the laboratory of an alien scientist. Clues solving the mystery of the alien scientists' work are hidden throughout the lab.

The Doane Observatory, with Chicago's largest public telescope

American Bar Association Museum of Law

321 N. Clark Street
312-988-6222
www.abanet.org/museum
Open: M–F, 10:00 AM–4:00 PM
Admission: Free

Housed in the national headquarters of the American Bar
Association, the Museum of Law has offered exhibits on the law
and legal issues since 1996. "America's Lawyer Presidents: From
Law Office to Oval Office" is featured, highlighting the careers
of Americas 25 lawyer-presidents from John Adams to Abraham
Lincoln to Bill Clinton. Grouped in chronological order as
Founding Fathers and Sons, Antebellum Presidents, Gilded Age
Presidents, New Century Presidents, and the Modern
Presidency, the exhibit documents the careers and challenges of
each president with film, graphics, and interactive computers.
Biographical information and anecdotes include portraits of the
young lawyers and reproductions of political cartoons, newspaper
articles, and letters detailing key cases. Visitors must show a
photo ID at the front desk before entering the museum.

Highlights:
An overview of Abraham Lincoln's 5,100 cases during his 25-
year career as a trial and appellate lawyer

A. Philip Randolph Pullman Porter Museum

10406 S. Maryland Avenue
773-928-3935
www.aphiliprandolphmuseum.org

Open: Th, F, Sa, 11:00 AM–4:00 PM (Apr–Dec 1)
Admission: $5

The legacy of A. Philip Randolph and contributions made by African Americans to Americas labor movement are celebrated in the A. Philip Randolph Pullman Porter Museum. Founded in 1995, the museum is located on Chicago's far south side in the historic Pullman district. The Chicago-based Pullman Palace Car Company was the largest single employer of black labor in the U.S., with approximately 12,000 African Americans working mostly as porters after World War I. After years of unfair wages and labor practices, the Pullman Porters organized the Brotherhood of Sleeping Car Porters in 1925 and asked A. Philip Randolph, a black New York journalist, to be their president. Under Randolph's leadership, the BSCP became the first African American labor union in the country to win a collective bargaining agreement in 1937. Exhibited are collections of photographs and memorabilia pertaining to A. Philip Randolph, the Pullman Porters, and historic Pullman district; as well as the Great Migration, American labor history, and the Civil Rights movement.

Archdiocese of Chicago's Joseph Cardinal Bernardin Archives and Records Center Museum

711 W. Monroe Street
312-831-0711
www.archives.archchicago.org
Open: M–F, 9:00 AM–5:00 PM
Admission: Free

A repository for the records of the Archdiocese of Chicago, the Joseph Cardinal Bernardin Archives and Records Center contains 8,000 cubic feet of mostly twentieth-century records. Included are the papers and photographs of Chicago cardinals, archbishops, bishops, and other former ordinaries of the diocese. Also among the holdings are Catholic Youth Organization and New World photograph collections, as well as sacramental registers, parish annual reports, liturgical and devotional materials, and student transcripts and yearbooks. The museum was established in 1997 with two galleries focusing on exhibits that showcase materials from the archives, and a third gallery devoted to Pope John Paul II and his 1979 visit to Chicago.

Highlights:
An enlarged photograph of the XXVIII International Eucharist Congress held at Soldier Field in 1926

Art Institute of Chicago

111 S. Michigan Avenue
312-443-3600
www.artic.edu

Open: M, Tu, W, F, 10:30 AM–4:30 PM; Th, 10:30 AM–8:30 PM; Sa &
Su, 10:00 AM–5:00 PM
Admission: Adults, $12; Seniors, Students, and Children, $7; Children
under 5, Free; Tuesdays Free; Some exhibitions require purchasing a
ticket

The Art Institute of Chicago was built at its present site to
house the international parliaments and public speeches associated with the World's Columbian Exposition. The classical Beaux
Arts-style building was constructed atop the rubble of the Great
Fire and opened to the public in 1893. Both a museum and a
school, it ranks as one of the city's grandest treasures and one of
the country's best art schools. Founded in 1866 as the Chicago
Academy of Design, the museum's earliest patrons traveled to
Europe to bring back paintings by the Old Masters,
Impressionists, and Postimpressionists. Since then, the permanent
collection has grown to over 300,000 works of art, and the
museum expanded to create more spacious galleries, including an
addition built over the Illinois Central Railroad tracks.

Best known for one of the most extensive collections of
Impressionist art outside of France, including one of the largest
collections of paintings by Claude Monet, the European
Collection includes work by Old Masters as well as Modernists
dating from the middle ages to the twentieth century. Arms and
armor from the fifteenth through nineteenth centuries include

standing suits of armor, horse gear, swords, daggers, and firearms. European decorative arts include furniture, ceramics, metalwork, glass, enamels, and ivory from the last 900 years and sculpture from the medieval period to 1900. The Thorne Rooms provide a glimpse of 68 miniature European and American interiors from the thirteenth century to the 1930s.

The African collection features works of wood sculpture, masks, ceramics, furniture, textiles, and beadwork from West, Central, and Southern Africa, while the Amerindian collection includes Mesoamerican, Andean, and South American ceramics, sculpture, textiles, and metalwork.

American paintings and sculpture from the eighteenth century to 1950 range from the landscapes and seascapes of Winslow Homer to the familiar cowboy art of Frederick Remington to abstract paintings by Georgia O'Keeffe.

Asian archaeological and artistic objects include Chinese jades and bronzes, Indian and Persian miniature paintings and sculpture, and one of the finest collections of Japanese wood block prints in the world.

The Department of Contemporary Art encompasses significant art movements from 1950 to the present, including painting, sculpture, and installation art by artists from all over the world. Departments of Photography, Prints and Drawings, Architecture and Design exhibit works in dedicated galleries.

The Kraft Education Center features interactive exhibits for children and hosts fun gallery games that encourage kids to participate in the museum experience.

Forming one of the largest art libraries in the world, the Ryerson Library and the Burnham Library of Architecture are open to qualified researchers or visitors with a referral from a local library.

Highlights:

Georges Seurat's *A Sunday on La Grande Jatte*

El Greco's *The Assumption of the Virgin* — his greatest work outside Spain

Grant Wood's *American Gothic*

Edward Hopper's *Nighthawks*

The largest collection of Joseph Cornell boxes on public display in the world

Balzekas Museum of Lithuanian Culture

6500 S. Pulaski Road
773-582-6500

Open: Daily, 10:00 AM–4:00 PM
Admission: Adults, $4; Seniors and Students, $3; Children, $1

The largest Lithuanian Museum outside of Lithuania, the Balzekas Museum of Lithuanian Culture, founded in 1966 on the Southwest side, traces the history and culture of the small Baltic state. "Lithuania Through the Ages," a permanent exhibit, transports visitors with an orientation video of green country-sides, seashores, and scenic castles and through antiquities, art, artifacts, books, photographs, arms and armor, maps and decorative ornaments, traces 1,000 years of events. Native costumes, amber jewelry, textiles, dolls, and decorated eggs are exhibited in the Women's Guild Room along with a display of famous Lithuanian women. In the Children's Museum of Immigration History, children from 2 to 12 can enter the "Castle Quest" exhibit by crossing over a drawbridge. Authentic chain mail worn by knights and a 4-foot armor jigsaw puzzle are featured as well as medieval-style costumes available for transformations into a king or princess. The museum also houses a photo archives and Lithuanian library containing genealogical records, monographs, and manuscripts.

Highlights:
A lovely collection of amber, often referred to as Lithuanian gold

Block Museum of Art

40 Arts Circle Drive, Northwestern University, Evanston
847-491-4000
www.blockmuseum.northwestern.edu

Open: Tu, 10:00 AM–5:00 PM; W–F, 10:00 AM–8:00 PM; Sa & Su,
Noon–5:00 PM
Admission: Free

Located on the lakefront campus of Northwestern University,
the Mary and Leigh Block Museum of Art was established in
1980. When Chicago art collectors Mary and Leigh Block
donated funds for a temporary exhibition and programming
space, the gallery became a repository for works of art given to
the university during the last century. A bequest of a group of
bronze outdoor sculptures by Leigh Block grew into an outdoor
sculpture garden containing 22 monumental sculptures by some
of the twentieth century's most renowned sculptors, including
Jean Arp, Barbara Hepworth, Henry Moore, Jaques Lipchitz,
and Joan Miro. As the permanent collection continued to grow,
the gallery became known as the Block Museum of Art in 1998.
An expanded state-of-the-art facility was opened in 2000,
including a print, drawing, and photography center to house and
exhibit the permanent collection of 4,000 works on paper.
Featured are post-1945 fine-arts prints, photographs documenting
American life from the 1940s to the present, American prints
made between the two world wars, prints by Chicago artists,
German Expressionist prints, eighteenth and nineteenth century
satirical prints from England and France, and Renaissance and
Baroque prints and drawings. Drawing work from the permanent
collection, the museum mounts four major scholarly exhibitions

and up to 10 smaller ones a year. Print, Drawing, and Photography Center collections are accessible by appointment only. The permanent collection is also viewable online.

Highlights:

Architectural drawings by Walter Burley and Marion Mahoney Griffen

Resting Leaf, a sculpture by Jean Arp

Bronzeville Children's Museum

9500 S. Western Avenue, Evergreen Park
708-636-9504
www.bronzevillechildrensmuseum.com

Open: Tu–Sa, 10:00 AM–4:00 PM, with weekday mornings reserved for
school groups
Admission: Adults, $3; Children, $2

Located on the south side in Evergreen Plaza shopping mall, the
museum is named after the historic Bronzeville neighborhood
where African Americans first settled following the Great
Migration from the South. Bronzeville quickly became the cultural hub for African Americans in the city and throughout the
country. Geared especially to underserved African American
children from 3 to 11, the museum was founded in 1993 by
Chicago civic leaders who saw the need for a child-friendly
museum to help increase literacy, hope, and self-esteem. Exhibits
highlighting the achievements of black pioneers, inventors,
explorers, musicians, and other important figures from local and
world history are rotated each year. Animated computer games,
colorful multipanel displays and sculpture, hands-on activities,
and play areas are tailored to each exhibit.

Cantigny Park

1 S. 151 Winfield Road, Wheaton
630-668-5161
www.mccormicktribune.org/cantigny

Open: Tu–Su, 10:00 AM–4:00 PM; –5:00 PM (Memorial Day–Labor Day); F, Sa, 10:00 AM–4:00 PM (Feb)
Admission: $7 per car during regular hours, $4 additional for twilight hours

Chicago publishing magnate Colonel Robert R. McCormick willed his 500-acre estate as a public park and recreation area in the town of Wheaton, 30 miles west of Chicago. Publisher and editor in chief of the *Chicago Tribune* from 1925 to 1955, he served as a commander in the First Infantry Division of the United States Army during World War I. Named Cantigny in honor of the first American battle of the war, the estate includes a Beaux Arts–style house museum, the First Infantry Division Museum and Research Center, an outdoor tank park, 40-acre formal garden, and recreational facilities. Built in 1896 by McCormick's grandfather, Joseph Medill, the first and second floors of the 35-room mansion are open for public tours and have been restored to reflect the way they looked between 1937 and 1955. Family heirlooms, Chinese and European works of art, and antique furniture are displayed, and period window dressings and upholstery have been reproduced. Opened in a converted stable in 1960, the First Infantry Division Museum and research center are now housed in a 38,000-square-foot facility that honors soldiers of the First Infantry from 1917 through Desert Storm. With 10,000 square feet of interactive and experiential exhibits, the museum also features dioramas depicting battle scenes and barracks that incorporate built-in cases containing artifacts. Exhibits include photographs and maps and recorded oral histories. An outdoor park contains tanks from World War II, the Korean War, and the Viet Nam War that children can climb on. The Robert R. McCormick Research Center contains reference books and periodicals on military history and service, microform records, and oral histories from First Division veterans. It also houses the Chicago Tribune Archives and materials related to journalism and freedom of the press.

Highlights:

Visitors are invited to board a simulated World War II landing craft headed for Omaha Beach, where a recording of a soldier's letter to his wife and children forms a montage with dramatic images of the invasion on a screen.

Charnley-Persky House

1365 N. Astor Street
312-915-0105
www.sah.org

Open: Tours available W, Noon; Sa, 10:00 AM and 1:00 PM (Apr–Nov);
10:00 AM (Dec–Mar); Saturday tours include the Madlener House
Admission: Charnley-Persky House tour only: Adults, $5; Seniors and
Students 18 and under, $3.50; Both houses: Adults, $10; Seniors and
Students age 18 and under, $5

Commissioned by lumberman James Charnley and his wife
Helen Douglas, the Charnley-Persky house was designed by
Louis Sullivan and his young draftsman, Frank Lloyd Wright, in
1891. Located on Chicago's Gold Coast within the historic
Astor Street district, the house sits in contrast with the surrounding high Victorian neighborhood. Claimed by Wright as
the "first modern house in America," the two architects rejected
Victorian-style ornamentation for abstract qualities and a façade
of plain limestone and Roman brick featuring a wood balcony.
The house interior is dominated by a dramatic atrium reaching
from the entryway to a third-story skylight with arched doorways
into rooms symmetrically located on each side. Rich oak paneling and fine carvings on the doors, balusters, and mantels combine stylized plant forms with geometrical patterns. The four-
bedroom house includes six baths and ventilated closets. Visitors
can't resist the urge to guess which architect was responsible for
prominent design features, but historians agree that the spatial
and ornamental experiments evident in the Charnley-Persky
House blossomed in the Prairie School designs of the next gen-
eration. Seymour Persky purchased the house for the Society of

Architectural Historians in 1995, and it was renamed in his honor. The offices of the society are now located on the second and third floors.

Highlights:

A delicate lattice screen that conceals the central stairs

A display in the butler's pantry of bottles and ceramic fragments found buried in the yard during restoration

Charles Gates Dawes House, Evanston Historical Society

225 Greenwood Street, Evanston
847-475-3410
www.evanstonhistorical.org

Open: Th–Su, 1:00 PM–5:00 PM
Admission: Adults, $5; Seniors, Students, and Children 6–18, $3;
Children under 6, Free

This 26-room mansion was built in 1896, and occupied by
Charles Gates Dawes, winner of the 1925 Nobel Peace Prize and
thirtieth vice president of the United States under Calvin
Coolidge, and his wife Caro Dawes from 1909 until their deaths.
Now headquarters of the Evanston Historical Society and
restored to its 1920s appearance, the chateau-like house features a
two-story great hall with a magnificent sprawling staircase and
ornate mahogany woodwork, a library lined with portraits of
ancestors and heirloom furniture, and a dining room with a
vaulted ceiling. Selections from the society's 10,000-piece collection of costumes from the 1850s to the present are exhibited in
the parlor on period mannequins, with a focus on fabric texture
and beauty. A second-floor nursery displays furniture and toys
that belonged to Mrs. Dawes and her children. Other upstairs
rooms serve as exhibit space, a research center, and offices.

Highlights:
Tiffany light fixtures throughout the house, including a stunning
chandelier with daffodil motif in the dining room

Chicago Children's Museum

700 E. Grand Avenue at Navy Pier
312-527-1000
www.chichildrensmuseum.org

Open: Tu–Su, 10:00 AM–5:00 PM; Th, 10:00 AM–8:00 PM
Admission: Children and Adults, $7; Seniors, $6; Children under 1, Free

With 57,000 square feet of exhibits, the Chicago Children's
Museum is the largest museum in town geared specifically for
kids. Founded by the Junior League of Chicago in 1982, the
museum moved to its present location on Navy Pier in 1995.
With three floors of hands-on activity designed for toddlers to
10 year olds, the museum contains 15 permanent exhibits and
learning adventures and hosts several temporary exhibits as well.
For preschoolers, a miniature cityscape, complete with a kid-
sized CTA bus, encourages role playing within a grocery store
equipped with plastic foods, carts, and a checkout stand. Small
children can don raincoats and discover the uses and benefits of
water by constructing fountains and dams in channels of moving
water. Dinosaur bones await excavation, an urban garden and
nature trail invite exploration, and science exhibits on recycling
and inventing inspire curiosity. Children and adults can learn
tools for addressing prejudice and discrimination in the multimedia exhibit Face to Face.

Highlights:
"The Big Backyard" hosts the Butterfly and Raindrop Screens:
interactive digital environments where children can add their
moving silhouettes to a nature scene using props or their bodies

Chicago Historical Society

Clark Street at North Avenue
312-642-4600
www.chicagohs.org

Open: M–Sa, 9:30 AM–4:30 PM; Su, Noon–5:00 PM
Admission: Adults, $5; Seniors and Students, 13–22, $3; Children, 6–12, $1

One of the oldest cultural institutions in the city, the Chicago Historical Society was founded in 1856 and today ranks at the top of the nation's urban historical museums. Established in Lincoln Park in 1932, the building interior incorporates a terra cotta arch designed by Daniel Burnham in the late 1800s, which once framed the entrance to the National Livestock Bank. In 1861 the secretary of the society wrote to president Abraham Lincoln to inform him of being elected an honorary member, and the museum began to collect and exhibit Lincolniana. With most of the Lincoln material now carefully preserved away from public view, new exhibits place Lincoln within a broad national context, exploring the institution of slavery and the devastation of the Civil War. Featured are Lincoln's letters and campaign materials, his spectacles, a life mask and cast hands, and the lodging house bed upon which he died. In the Chicago galleries, the city's dramatic past is explored through subjects like Fort Dearborn and frontier Chicago, the Great Fire, the Haymarket Riot, the stockyards that gave Chicago reason to proclaim itself "Hog Butcher to the World," and the World's Columbian Exposition of 1893. In addition, the stories of contemporary everyday Chicagoans are told through video and artifacts in "Out of the Loop." A dynamic special exhibition program celebrates

Chicago's heritage with changing exhibits. The society houses one of the city's best public research facilities with over 20 million items, including photographs, drawings, diaries, letters, costumes, textiles, sound recordings and films, books and newspapers, and many other artifacts

Highlights:

Chicago's first locomotive, the 160-year old *Pioneer*, which kids can climb aboard

Selections from the Hope B. McCormick Costume Center, featuring 50,000 pieces, with the earliest dating from the late eighteenth century.

A horse-drawn carriage used by President Lincoln

Chinese-American Museum of Chicago

238 West 23rd Street
312-949-1000
www.ccamuseum.org

Open: F–Su, 11:30 AM–5:00 PM
Admission: Call ahead for information

Celebrating Chinese-American cultural heritage in the
Midwest, the Chinese-American Museum opened in 2005 in a
4-story landmark-status building constructed in 1896. Originally
a warehouse with shop space downstairs, it is located in the
heart of Chicago's Chinatown and served as the headquarters of
the Quong Yick Wholesale Trading Company for half a century. The second largest Chinese foodstuff wholesaler in the
Midwest, Quong Yick grew bean sprouts in the basement and
made its own bean curd. A permanent collection of several hun-
dred objects and the mini-dioramas from the Ling Long
Museum, formerly located in the neighborhood, make up the
core. Dioramas depict popular historical subjects relating to
family, bravery, and loyalty. Two floors of exhibits also feature
old-style garments and photographs that capture the day-to-day
aspects of Chinatown. Rare documents with illustrations and
computer interactives are included. "Paper Sons" highlights the
passage and lifestyles of Chinese immigrants to Chicago
between 1870 and 1945.

Highlights:
A reconstruction of a 1930s Chinese laundry

Clarke House Museum

1827 S. Indiana Avenue
312-326-1480

Guided tours: W–Su, Noon, 1:00 PM, 2:00 PM
Admission: Adults, $10; Seniors, $8; Children 5–12, $5; Glessner House
tour included: Adults, $15; Seniors, $11; Children, $8

In 1836, a year before Chicago was incorporated as a city and
while Fort Dearborn still stood on the banks of the Chicago
River, Henry and Caroline Clarke began building their home.
Their Greek Revival house, the oldest home in Chicago, originally stood on 20 acres of lakefront land but wasn't finished until
after Henry's death in 1849 when Caroline sold part of the property to have money to raise their children. In 1872 the house was
sold and moved 30 blocks south, then purchased by the City of
Chicago in 1977 and returned near where it originally stood. The
move required the use of jacks to raise it above the elevated train
tracks, which by then stood in the way. With restoration com-
pleted in 2004, the house was outfitted with 1850s period furniture and fixtures. Today, in the Prairie Avenue historic district,
the Clarke House serves as a museum of middle class family life
in early Chicago. A second-floor gallery displays photographs of
the house's history, a scale model, and a hands-on example of
mortise-and-tenon joinery used in building the house. A garden
featuring fruit trees, winding paths, and flowers is recreated in the
yard, which was dedicated as the Millennium Park for Women
by First Lady Hillary Clinton.

Tours begin next door at the Glessner House Museum coach
house, and tickets can be purchased there.

Highlights:

A combination rocking chair and cradle

Chairs and settees with no armrests which accommodated ladies' full skirts

Period costumes on display in the parlor

D. L. Moody Museum

820 N. LaSalle Avenue
312-329-4404
www.moody.edu

Open: M–F, 7:00 AM–5:30 PM; Sa, 10:00 AM–4:00 PM
Admission: Free

The D. L. Moody Museum, located on the campus of the
Moody Bible Institute, tells the story of the inspired life and
career of founder Dwight Lyman Moody, one of the most successful evangelists of the nineteenth century. Moody came from
a childhood of poverty and reached financial success as a shoe
salesman but gave up prosperity when he became "born again"
into the ministry of Christ. After moving to Chicago in the
mid-1880s, he was drawn to work with the poor in the slums of
"little Hell" and by 1860 had attracted a Sunday-school following of over 1,500. He ministered to soldiers in the Civil War, led
extensive evangelistic campaigns throughout America and Great
Britain, and served as president of the YMCA. In 1886 he
founded what is now known as the Moody Bible Institute. The
museum offers a 15-minute video on the life and work of D. L.
Moody and interactive displays that mix recordings of dramatic
readings about his work with artifacts from his life, including the
Bible he used to preach with.

Highlights:
An early recording of Moody reciting the Beatitudes
A tableau of items from Moody's office, including desk, walking
cane, and his favorite teacup.

DuSable Museum of African-American History

740 East 56th Place
773-947-0600
www.dusablemuseum.org

Open: M–Sa, 10:00 AM–5:00 PM; Su, Noon–5:00 PM
Admission: Adults, $3; Seniors and Students, $2; Children 6–13, $1,
Children under 6, Free; Sundays, Free

Known as the Ebony Museum when founded in 1961, the museum's original site was in the home of its founders, artist and educator Margaret Goss Burroughs and her husband Charles Burroughs. It was the first museum in the nation dedicated to African and African American history and culture. As a result of a community campaign, the museum took up new residence under its current name in a park administration building located in the South Side's Washington Park in 1973. Named in honor of Jean Baptist Point DuSable, a black fur trader who in 1779 was the first permanent non-Native settler in what became Chicago, the museum is a repository of 13,000 artifacts, books, photographs, art objects, and memorabilia pertaining to the African American experience. Included in the collection are the diaries of sea explorer Captain Harry Dean and letters, photographs, and memorabilia of W. E. B. Du Bois and Langston Hughes. On permanent display are a collection of African masks, oil paintings, and sculpture of bronze, stone and terra cotta by African American artists dating mostly from the WPA and Civil Rights eras. A graphic exhibit on slavery and segregation contains slave shackles and reproductions of posters advertising slave auctions and rewards for runaway slaves. Photographs of lynchings and "for whites only" public signage are reminders of a painful past. An exhibit on Harold Washington, Chicago's first African American mayor, tells his story with graphics, memorabilia, and personal effects; and the achievements of black aviators from the Tuskegee Airmen to Major Robert H. Lawrence, the nation's first African American astronaut, are celebrated. As part of its programming, the museum hosts traveling exhibits that address black issues and historical events as well as the lives of renowned African American leaders and artists.

Highlights:

A spectacular cast bronze equestrian statue from Cameroon
Oil paintings by Augustus Savage, Henry O. Tanner, and Chicago artists Archibald Motley, Charles Sebree, and Marion Perkins.

Elks Veterans Memorial

2750 North Lakeview Avenue
773-755-4876
www.elks.org/memorial

Open: M–F, 9:00 AM–5:00 PM; Sa & Su, 10:00 AM–5:00 PM (Apr 15–Nov 15)
Admission: Free

The Elks National Veterans Memorial and Headquarters opened in 1926 to honor the Elks who served the country in World War I. Designed by New York architect Egerton Swartwout, it was rededicated in subsequent years to honor members who served in World War II, the Korean War, Vietnam, Panama, Grenada, and Desert Storm. The classical domed building has a striking presence in its Lincoln Park location near the lakefront. Columns line the circumference of the limestone exterior, with niches displaying bronze sculpture representing Liberty and Family and the Ages of Man, while bronze elks flank the entrance. The interior rotunda features four gold leaf-covered statues representing principles of charity, justice, brotherly love, and fidelity and columns and a floor made of six varieties of marble from around the world. Allegorical murals and intricately designed art glass adorn the walls of the rotunda and adjoining grand reception room. The building houses the office of the Elks' Grand Exalted Ruler and conference rooms with 1868 photographs of the original Elks organization, then called "The Jolly Corks," and displays of ribbons and medals. Basement exhibits of memorabilia are also on view.

Highlights:
Art Deco murals painted by Eugene F. Savage

Elmhurst Art Museum

150 Cottage Hill Avenue, Elmhurst
630-834-0202
www.elmhurstartmuseum.org

Open: Tu, Th, Sa, 10:00 AM–4:00 PM; W, 1:00 PM–8:00 PM; F, Su, 1:00
PM–4:00 PM
Admission: Adults, $4; Seniors, $3; Students, $2; Children under 12,
free

The Elmhurst Art Museum, located 15 miles west of Chicago,
was established in 1980 and formerly housed in the Elmhurst
Community Center. In 1991 the museum purchased the
McCormick House, one of only three homes in the U.S.
designed and built by Mies van der Rohe, and moved it to
Wilder Park, where a new museum would be built around it.
Designed according to Meisien ideals of light and space by
DeStefano & Partners with glass and steel curtain walls, the
museum was nationally recognized for architectural excellence at
its opening in 1997. Temporary exhibitions of work by regional
mid-career artists are regularly featured at the museum, which also
hosts national shows. EAM houses an eclectic permanent collection of twentieth-century paintings, including works by Sonia
Delaunay and Marc Chagall, prints, and outdoor sculpture.

Highlights:
The McCormick House, built in 1952 of brick, glass and steel,
resembles a one-story slice of the skyscrapers designed by Mies
van der Rohe

Ernest Hemingway Birthplace House

339 North Oak Park Avenue, Oak Park
708-848-2222
www.ehfop.org

Open: Su–F, 1:00 PM–5:00 PM; Sa, 10:00 AM–5:00 PM
Admission: Adults $7; Seniors and Children 18 and under, $5.50;
Children under 5, free

Ernest Hemingway was born in 1899 in Oak Park, Illinois, in a
house built by his maternal grandparents. The Queen
Anne–style house, replete with Victorian wallpaper, period furniture, paintings, decorations, and utensils, was restored in 1994
and made into a museum. The home and furnishings paint a portrait of the middle-class lifestyle of the large Hemingway family
until Ernest turned 6 years old. Included are items representing
his father's profession as a doctor, naturalist, and photographer
and his mother's vocation as a music teacher. The elder
Hemingway's photographs adorn most of the walls of the house.
Docents provide tours with biographical information and anecdotes about the family. A map of other Hemingway sites in the
neighborhood is available.

Highlights:
Vivid stories of Ernest's parents and grandparents and their influ-
ence on the family
Framed nursery illustrations of toddlers (including one named
Humphrey) by the mother of Humphrey Bogart, a family friend

Ernest Hemingway Museum

200 North Oak Park Avenue, Oak Park
708-848-2222
www.ehfop.org

Open: Su–F, 1:00 PM–5:00 PM; Sa, 10:00 AM–5:00 PM
Admission: Adults, $7; Seniors and Children 18 and under, $5.50;
Children 5 and under, free; also free with admission to Ernest
Hemingway Birthplace House

Less than two blocks away from his birthplace, the Ernest
Hemingway Museum focuses on the first 20 years of the writer's
life in Oak Park and his hometown's impact on his later life and
work. Beginning with pencil drawings by Hemingway as a 2 year
old and descriptions of his early love for nature, the exhibit con-
tinues with a classroom tableau, and a discussion about the high
school English teachers who recognized his talent early. A timeline documents his dramatic adult life, work, friendships and
influences. Included are photographs of Hemingway as a World
War I ambulance driver, a correspondent in World War II, his
Paris years, and his glamorous pursuits as an outdoorsman. Video
displays feature film footage of Hemingway and accounts of his
life given by family members and friends. Nearly five decades of
work are also discussed.

Highlights:
Videos of 15 movies made from his stories available for viewing
Photograph of young Ernest fishing, taken by his father in 1905

Field Museum of Natural History

1400 S. Lake Shore Drive
312-922-9410
www.fieldmuseum.org

Open: Daily, 9:00 AM–5:00 PM
Admission: Adults, $19; Seniors, $14; Students, $14; Children 4–11, $9
(Check for discount days and package deals)

Founded in 1894 to house the anthropological and biological collections of the World's Columbian Exposition, the museum, known then as the Columbian Museum of Chicago, was located in the south side's Jackson Park. Honoring benefactor Marshall Field, the name was changed to the Field Museum, and in 1921 it moved to its present neoclassical home in Grant Park. The Field is one of three major public institutions situated on the Museum Campus, less than a mile southeast of the Loop, with a panoramic view of Lake Michigan and the Chicago skyline. With more than 70 scientists on staff exploring cultures and environments from around the world, it is one of the finest natural history museums in the world and one of the city's most popular attractions. At 65 million years old, the largest and most complete *Tyrannosaurus rex* ever found (known as Sue), greets visitors in the grand and light-filled Stanley Field Hall. Large galleries branching off the main hall contain nine acres of immersive, interactive, and scholarly exhibitions. Housing over 20 million specimens in its collection, exhibitions include fossils that tell the story of our evolving planet, artifacts from the ancient Americas beginning with the mammoth hunters of North America, and animal kingdom exhibits exploring issues in biology. Africa and Pacific exhibits showcase objects from anthropology collections and create environments for visualizing ways of human and animal life. Twenty-three mummies and a recreated mastaba are exhibited in "Inside Ancient Egypt" along with an authentic royal barge, and a living marsh with papyrus. Children especially will enjoy "Life Underground," where visitors are invited shrink to a size smaller than a penny and experience life in the soil with giant robotic insects and hands-on activities. Laboratories with glass walls are built into exhibits so visitors can watch museum preparators meticulously clean dinosaur fossils for study and carefully conserve artifacts. Major traveling exhibits with wide-ranging themes are mounted several times a year. The museum also houses a natural history library with 275,000 volumes, a rare-book room, photo archives, and a periodical collection. The public may visit the library on weekdays by contacting a Protection Services officer at any museum entrance.

Highlights:

Full-scale reproduction of a traditional Pawnee earth lodge, a fully furnished Native America dwelling that brings to life the traditional ways of the Great Plains tribe

Carved wooden totem poles and painted masks from Pacific Northwest Coast Indians

A shrine to the Egyptian cat goddess Bastet and a mini diorama depicting mummification and burial techniques of ancient Egypt

Stunning selections from museum collections in the Grainger Gallery

A collection of bronze Benin heads and objects from West Africa

Frank Lloyd Wright Home and Studio

951 Chicago Avenue, Oak Park
708-848-1976
www.wrightplus.org

Open: Tours available M–F, 11:00 AM, 1:00 PM, 3:00 PM; Sa & Su, every 20 minutes from 11:00 AM–3:30 PM

Admission: Adults, $9; Seniors and Children 7–18, $7

The world's largest concentration of buildings designed by Americas most influential architect, Frank Lloyd Wright, exists in Oak Park, 10 miles west of Chicago. There in his home and studio, which he designed in 1889 at age 22, is where he and his wife Catherine Tobin spent 20 years raising six children. The Prairie style of architecture was conceived in this house, and while it did not originally exemplify the Prairie style, ideas leading up to it are discernable in the features of both the home and studio. After extensive restoration beginning in 1974, the brick and shingled home and studio were opened as a museum that also contains extensive woodwork, leaded glass windows, furniture and light fixtures designed by Wright for the home. Pieces from his personal art collection and utilitarian items from his studio are also on display. The docent-led tour provides personal information about Wright, his family, and work. Tours for children 6–12 are also available.

Highlights:
Hidden piano in the children's second-floor playroom
Octagonal studio containing a loft supported by a chain and harness system instead of conventional beams

Gerber/Hart Gay and Lesbian Library and Archives

1127 W. Granville Avenue
773-381-8030
www.gerberhart.org
Open: W, Th, 6:00 PM–9:00 PM; F–Su, Noon–4:00 PM (Library);
Archives and Special Collections by appointment only
Admission: Free

A repository for the records of lesbian, gay, bisexual, and trans-gendered individuals and organizations, the Gerber/Hart Library and Archives was founded in 1981 as a joint project of the Gay Academic Union- Chicago Chapter, Gay Horizons, and the Chicago Gay and Lesbian History Project. Named after 1920s Chicago activist Henry Gerber and civil liberties attorney Pearl Hart, the library is located in a 5,000-square-foot double store-front in the Edgewater neighborhood. It is the largest LGBT circulating library in the Midwest, with more than 14,000 volumes, 800 periodical titles, 100 archival collections, and sound and visual recordings. Materials document national and international groups, with particular emphasis on the Midwest and the political development of Chicago's LGBT community. In addition to preserving community materials, the library seeks to be a conduit for change. Special Collections accessible by appointment include exhibits of T-shirts, buttons, posters, and ephemera recording local and national LGBT organizations. Pre-1969 periodicals are included along with international journals and newsweeklies from over 100 cities and 24 countries and rare, early histories and novels.

Glessner House Museum

1800 S. Prairie Avenue
312-326-1480
www.glessnerhouse.org

Open: Guided tours W–Su at 1:00 PM, 2:00 PM, 3:00 PM
Admission: Adults, $10; Students and Seniors, $8; Children 5–12, $5
For tours that include the Clarke House: Adults, $15, Students and
Seniors, $11; Children 5–12, $8

After the Civil War, Prairie Avenue was home to some of the
century's great industrial magnates and was the most fashionable
street in Chicago. In 1887 John and Frances Glessner moved into
their new 19,000-square-foot home, which was designed by
Boston architect Henry Hobson Richardson and staffed with
eight servants. A radical departure from Victorian architecture,
the house was considered an "urban masterpiece" with a
Romanesque, fortress-like granite exterior and an oak-paneled
English Arts and Crafts interior featuring furniture and picture
frames by Isaac Scott, wallpaper and textiles by William Morris
& Co, and hundreds of Aesthetic and English Arts and Crafts
movement decorative objects. Serving as an inspiration to young
Frank Lloyd Wright, the architecture and furnishings of the
Glessner home helped redefine residential design and urban living. Purchased and restored by the city of Chicago, the house
museum is furnished today with items nearly all original to the
Glessner family. Restored architectural features include an elegant central staircase with ornate balusters, a gold-leafed dining
room ceiling, a butler's pantry with copper sink, shellac-sealed
walls, and an enunciation system, and a special outside entrance
directly into cold storage for the ice man. Family photographs

are on display in a second-floor bedroom, and Frances' detailed journal writings describing many years of life in her home are in the collection at the Chicago Historical Society.

Highlights:

John Glessner's study with wood paneling, an enormous custom-made desk, his original library of hundreds of books, and numerous etchings, each with a uniquely carved wood frame.

A death mask of Lincoln's face and hands, rest on the desk.

Harold Washington Library Center

400 S. State Street
312-747-4300
www.chipublib.org

Open: M–Th, 9:00 AM–7:00 PM; F, Sa, 9:00 AM–5:00 PM; Su, 1:00
PM–5:00 PM
Admission: Free

The Harold Washington Library Center, named after Chicago's
first African American mayor, opened in 1991 and is the largest
public library building in the world. Designed by Thomas H.
Beeby and colleagues, the neoclassical building located in the
south loop is well known for its dramatically large sculpted owl
and seedpod roof ornaments. The forty-second mayor of
Chicago, Harold Washington was elected to office in 1983 and
served until his death in 1987. He is remembered for his accom-
plishments in a permanent exhibition, "Called to the Challenge:
The Legacy of Harold Washington," located on the library's
ninth floor. Featured are photographs, letters, newspaper clippings, election memorabilia, and a timeline of his life. Visitors
can select to listen to audio recordings of his most famous
speeches. Four to five exhibitions drawn from the library's Special
Collections and Preservation Division hall are mounted each
year in the Special Collections gallery. Materials include photographs and artifacts of the Civil War, acquired by the library in
1948 from the Grand Army of the Republic Museum, and items
pertaining to Chicago history, including the Chicago Blues
Archives. Exhibitions are also mounted in the third-floor
Chicago gallery, and three to four traveling exhibits a year are
presented in the main gallery on the lower level. Works of art by

established and emerging Chicago artists from the City of Chicago's art collection are displayed throughout the library.

Highlights:

Audio recordings of Harold Washington's speeches

General Custer's hat

Audio and visual recordings of past and present blues performers and blues-related memorabilia

Health World

1301 S. Grove Avenue, Barrington
847-842-9100
www.healthworldmuseum.org

Open: Tu–Sa, 10:00 AM–3:00 PM
Admission: Children and Adults, $6; Children under 2, Free

Offering a creative learning environment that supplements health education efforts of schools, families, and health-care organizations, Health World was founded in 1995. Located in Barrington, 20 miles northwest of Chicago, the museum offers hands-on opportunities to learn more about the importance of leading a healthy lifestyle. Through state-of-the-art exhibits, including "Grossology," children learn about functions and quirks of the human body. Demonstrations throughout the day teach children and adults such life saving procedures as the Heimlich maneuver with the aid of "Choking Charlie." Other demonstrations for fire safety or on the digestive tract give children opportunities to learn safe practices and the importance of maintaining a good diet and exercise. The museum also provides a craft area and a replicated oak forest for exploration.

Hellenic Museum and Cultural Center

801 W. Adams Street
312-655-1234
www.hellenicmuseum.org

Open: Tu–F, 10:00 AM–4:00 PM
Admission: $5

Greek immigration to Chicago began after the Great Fire of 1871 when the rebuilding of the city provided many jobs. The migration wave peaked between 1900 and 1920, and Chicago became the largest community of Greeks in the U.S. until World War II. The Hellenic Museum and Cultural Center is located on the near west side, in what was once known as the "Greek Delta," where an enclave community lived and worked. The museum houses a permanent retrospective exhibit, "Remembering Generations: The Greek Immigrant's Journey," highlighting items from the collection that chronicle the paths of Greek immigrants and their assimilation into all facets of life in the United States. In a small gallery a suitcase and open trunk reveal hand made personal and ethnic articles like those carried by immigrants in the early twentieth-century, including an embroidered fez and belt with filigree buckle, a hand-woven tagari bag, linens, and a tiny pair of child's shoes. Traditional folk costumes, household items, and journals are also displayed. Adjoining galleries host rotating exhibits pertaining to Greek history and culture.

Highlights:
Religious ceremonial items from an early twentieth-century Greek Orthodox Church
A pair of hand-made beeswax bridal crowns

International Museum of Surgical Science

1524 N. Lake Shore Drive
312-642-6502
www.imss.org

Open: Tu–Sa, 10:00 AM–4:00 PM; Tu–Su (May–Sep)
Admission: Adults, $6; Seniors and Students, $3

Designed in 1917 by Howard Van Doren Shaw and modeled after a French chateau, the International Museum of Surgical Science is the only Gold Coast mansion open to the public. A division of the International College of Surgeons, the four-story museum opened in 1952 and contains over 7,000 artifacts spanning 4,000 years of surgical history. Permanent exhibits on surgery and its related sciences cover anesthesia, radiology, orthopedics, urology, cardiology, and ophthalmology. Antique surgical and medical implements such as a sixteenth-century Austrian amputation saw with reversible blade, surgical tools from the Civil War, early radiology equipment and X-rays, and a working iron lung are of special interest. A collection of turn-of-the-century apothecary jars and equipment are displayed, as well as a reproduction of a twentieth-century dentist's office. Pioneers of medical practice and important events in medical history are depicted in over 600 paintings, prints and sculpture throughout the museum. Contemporary artwork with medical themes is displayed in a rotating exhibition program.

Highlights:
Trepanning tools along with 4,000-year-old trepanned skulls excavated in Peru
A collapsible stethoscope designed to be carried in a top hat

Intuit: The Center for Intuitive and Outsider Art

756 N. Milwaukee Avenue
312-243-9088
www.art.org

Open: W–Sa, Noon–5:00 PM
Admission: Free

Chicago is a national center for the exhibition and interpretation of self-taught art. Intuit was formed in 1991 by a group of artists and collectors to recognize the creative work of individuals who are motivated by unique personal visions without the influence of the mainstream art world. Outsider Art was influential in the development of the work of many Chicago Imagists from 1945 to the 1970s. With two galleries for rotating exhibits and a performance space, the Center moved to its present near-west location in 1998 and began acquiring a permanent collection in 2002. Items from the collection and special exhibitions include paintings, drawings, and photographs. Scrapbooks, collages made with mosaic and glass fragments, found treasures, wood and concrete sculpture and yarn-wrapped objects are displayed as well as weathered components from monumental outdoor sculptural environments. The Darger Collection consists of assembled furniture, appliances, and artwork from the one-room home of Chicago native and self-taught artist Henry Darger. Special exhibitions include solo and group exhibits by self-taught artists and exhibits contrasting their work with the work of artists recognized by the art world.

Irish American Heritage Center

4626 N. Knox Avenue
773-282-7035
www.irishamhc.com

Open: By appointment, M–F, 9:00 AM–5:00 PM; Sa, 10:00 AM–4:00 PM
Admission: Free

In 1860 Chicago was home to the fourth largest Irish community in America. The Irish transformed Chicago from what was once a frontier prairie town to a thriving commercial and industrial center by the end of the nineteenth century. Twelve Irish mayors governed the city for more than 80 years, and Irish Americans continue to demonstrate their influence on St. Patrick's Day when attendance is still required by politicians in annual parades. The Irish American Heritage Center houses a small museum commemorating the Irish experience in Chicago. Artifacts and memorabilia include a replica of the *Book of Kells*, and a set of traditional Irish music books written by Captain Francis O'Neil, chief of police in Chicago from 1901 to 1905. Featured is an ornately carved wooden chair commissioned by the Irish Fellowship Club of Chicago to commemorate the visit of President William Howard Taft on Saint Patrick's Day in 1910. Also exhibited is a collection of Carrickmacross lace and a tapestry by Lily Yeats, sister of William Butler Yeats. A library of resources pertaining to the Irish experience worldwide is open to the public by appointment, and on weekend evenings the center operates a traditional Irish Pub.

Highlights:
A magnificent collection of Belleek Parian china

Jane Addams Hull–House Museum

800 S. Halsted, at the University of Illinois at Chicago
312-413-5353
www.uic.edu/jaddams/hull/newdesign/visiting

Open: Tu–F, 10:00 AM–4:00 PM; Su, Noon–4:00 PM
Admission: Free

The nation's most influential Settlement House, Hull-House was established by Jane Addams and Ellen Gates Starr in 1889. What began as a mansion expanded to a 13-building complex in a neighborhood of factories and tenements, where immigrants of 19 nationalities lived within a few blocks of each other. Hull-House provided social, educational, and artistic programs for thousands of neighborhood residents as well as daycare for working mothers and the first public playground. Addams and associates fought to reform child labor laws and occupational health and safety practices and lobbied for protection of women, children, and immigrants. Supporting women's suffrage, the Pacifist movement, and the creation of the NAACP and ACLU, she helped found the Women's Peace Party during World War I, and in 1931 won a Nobel Peace Prize for her work. The Hull-House Museum is a permanent memorial to its founder and consists of the mansion and one of the original 13 buildings. Located on the University of Illinois campus, the the mansion contains many of the original furnishings, photographs, artifacts from Hull-House programs, and a model of the Settlement House complex.

Highlights:
Artifacts of trades taught at the house, including pottery

Labor History Museum of the Illinois Labor History Society

28 E. Jackson Boulevard
312-663-4107
www.kentlaw.edu/ilhs/museum

Open: M–F, 9:30 AM–3:30 PM
Admission: Free

Organized in 1969 in the office of Chicago labor lawyer Joe Jacobs, the Illinois Labor History Society was founded to preserve knowledge of the people and events surrounding the formation of organized labor in Chicago. As industries grew and thrived in the late nineteenth century, workers all over the country were forced to spend long hours under poor conditions for meager wages. Collective bargaining power gained through unionization radically improved the lives of workers but was hard won. The society's collection includes photographs, documents, posters, and memorabilia commemorating the history of organized labor in Chicago and houses a reference library of biographies of people with connections to labor politics and other labor-related books. The museum opened to the public in 1997 with a modest display, including a brick from the street under the speaker's podium at the Haymarket demonstration on May 4, 1886; photographs of Joe Hill's west-side funeral procession in 1915; and the violent confrontation between Chicago police and Republic Steel strikers in 1937.

Highlights:
An 1886 white dress uniform of the Bohemian Butchers Protective Association

Latvian Folk Art Museum

4146 N. Elston Avenue
773-588-2085

Open: Daily, 10:00 AM–1:00 PM, or by appointment
Admission: Free

Recognizing the need to preserve their heritage, Osvald Grins and daughter Astra Revelins, founding Chicago Latvian Association members, traveled around the United States in the 1960s, visiting Latvian immigrants who donated or loaned important artifacts for an archive. In 1978 the Latvian Folk Art Museum opened on the second floor of the Latvian Community Center on the west side of Chicago with the archive materials forming the core of a collection that was supplemented by Chicago and regional members of the community. Latvian immigrants began arriving in Chicago in small numbers in the late nineteenth century, seeking change from hardships endured while Latvia was a part of the Russian empire. The country declared independence in 1918, and emigration ceased until after World War II, when Latvia fell to Stalin's rule. Fleeing Soviet occupation, many settled in Chicago. When the country regained its independence in 1991, some returned, leaving Chicago with a population of 6,000 Latvians today. The small museum focuses on many beautiful hand-woven wool textiles, including women's folk attire, blankets, and sagsas (large, often embroidered shoulder scarves). Reproductions of ceramics made in the style of Latgale and decorated with incised lines and fluting are also featured. The collection includes hand-made musical instruments such as the kokle (traditional stringed instrument), wooden trumpets, horns, and whistles carved from twigs.

Spinning wheels and a small loom complement the woven pieces, and a large collection of hand-knit mittens with intricate designs are displayed.

Highlights:
A reproduction of an eleventh- to twelfth-century woman's ceremonial costume from Latgale along with jewelry excavated from an ancient burial site

Leather Archives and Museum

6418 N. Greenview Avenue
773-761-9200
www.leatherarchives.org

Open: Th, Noon–8:00 PM; Sa & Su, Noon–3:00 PM and by special arrangement

Admission: Adults suggested donation, $5

For adults only, the Leather Archives and Museum was incorporated in 1991 and grew out of exhibits at the International Mr. Leather conventions in Chicago. Celebrating the S&M/Leathers lifestyle, the museum opened in 2000 in its current location, which was formerly a community arts center, with 2,300 square feet of exhibit space in the main gallery. Featured in the museum are a timeline of S&M/Leathers culture from the earliest historical influences to present day icons. Exhibits of explicit erotic paintings, prints, and photographs, a leather bar tableau with boot blacking case, club memorabilia, black leather jackets, handcuffs, chains, and other S&M paraphernalia are displayed. Most images are oriented toward gay males. Archival materials include local and national organization and networking records and are available for research by appointment only.

Highlights:

Large-scale homoerotic oil paintings originally from The Gold Coast Bar by artist Etienne

Lizzadro Museum of Lapidary Arts

220 Cottage Hill Avenue, Elmhurst
630-833-1616
www.lizzadromuseum.org

Open: Tu–Sa, 10:00 AM–5:00 PM; Su, 1:00 PM–5:00 PM
Admission: Adults, $4; Seniors, $3; Students and Children 8–18, $2;
Children under 7, Free; Fridays, Free

Located In Wilder Park of suburban Elmhurst, 16 miles west of the Loop, the Lizzadro Museum of Lapidary Arts is one of the only museums devoted solely to the lapidary arts (the polishing and cutting of stones). Founded in 1962 with the collection of hobbyist Joseph F. Lizzadro, it includes 233 pieces of jade and hard stone carvings, snuff bottles, modern and antique vases, bowls, and decorative accessories. Collections of gemstones and minerals are displayed, along with examples of Florentine and Roman stone mosaics, gemstone cameos, and intaglios. Children will enjoy small dioramas featuring carved stone animals and the miniature Castle Lizzadro, finely crafted of gold and enhanced with mineral specimens. Visitors can also view meteorites, fluorescent rocks and minerals, bending rock, fossils, and birthstones.

Highlights:
A nephrite jade altar set from the Ming Dynasty
Carved gemstone-encrusted cinnabar screen, said to have been a gift to Chinese Emperor Qianlong in 1791

Loop Sculpture Tour

Downtown Chicago: Dearborn Street on the east, LaSalle Avenue on the west, Washington Street on the north, and Jackson Street on the south
www.ci.chi.il.us/tourism

Open: All hours
Admission: Free

From monuments by Loredo Taft to *Batcolumn* by Claus Oldenburg, more than 20 major public sculptures are installed throughout the downtown Chicago area known as the Loop. A more complete Loop Sculpture Guide is available at the Chicago Cultural Center at 78 E. Washington Street. Below are five of the most popular and accessible sculptures by some of the twentieth century's greatest artists.

"Untitled Picasso," Pablo Picasso, 1967 (Corten steel, 162 tons, 50 feet tall); Daley Plaza at Dearborn and Washington
A composition of weathered steel plates and rods resembling the abstracted head of a woman.

Monument with Standing Beast, Jean Dubuffet, 1989 (fiberglass, 10 tons, 29 feet tall); James R. Thompson Center at Randolph and Clark
An environmental sculpture composed of four white elements, painted with bold black lines, installed on the Helmut Jahn-designed Thompson Center plaza.

Chicago, Jean Miro, 1981 (steel, wire mesh, concrete, bronze, and ceramic tile, 10 tons, 39 feet tall); 69 West Washington

A stylized shape of a woman with a bronze headdress and concrete-mosaic skirt.

The Four Seasons, Marc Chagall, 1974 (hand-chipped stone and glass fragments set into cement; 3000 cubic feet, 10 feet tall); First National Plaza, Monroe between Dearborn and Clark
A massive, five-sided mosaic depicting six fanciful views of Chicago in all four seasons.

Flamingo, Alexander Calder, 1974 (steel, 53 feet tall); Federal Plaza, Dearborn between Jackson and Adams
Bright red steel plates with ribs and gussets forming two large arches with delicate bases that complement the Mies van der Rohe–designed post office on the plaza

Madlener House

4 Burton Place
312-573-1365
www.grahamfoundation.org

Open: 10:00 AM and 1:00 PM (Apr–Nov); 10:00 AM (Dec–Mar); available with Charnley-Persky House tours
Admission: Adults, $10; Seniors and Students 18 and under, $5 (both houses)

A few doors away from the Charnley-Persky House on the Gold Coast, Albert Fridolin Madlener and his wife Elsa Seipp Madlener commissioned E. Schmidt and Hugh M. G. Garden to design their home in 1901. The Madleners and Schmidt both came from prominent Chicago families that emigrated from Germany in the 1850s. The house demonstrates the amalgamation of traditional German neoclassical architecture with the innovation of what would become the Prairie style. By the turn of the century, Louis Sullivan was a central figure in a new architectural movement in Chicago toward simplification of form and unity of aesthetic and functional elements. The influence of Sullivan and Frank Lloyd Wright is seen in the overall severity of design of the Madlener House with the combination of natural and geometric ornaments, rich wood trim, deeply veined marble, and green and gold glass as decorative elements. Purchased and restored by the Graham Foundation in 1963, minor alterations were made to the interior to accommodate the foundation's philanthropic and educational activities. A permanent collection of fragments from famous Chicago buildings, many of them designed by Sullivan, was installed in the courtyard in 1987.

Martin D'Arcy Museum of Art

6525 N. Sheridan Road
773-508-2679
www.darcy.luc.edu

Open: Tu–Sa, Noon–4:00 PM; Tu, W, Th, Noon–4:00 PM (Jun–Sep)
Admission: Free

One of the largest Jesuit universities in the United States, Loyola University was founded in Chicago in 1870 and moved to its Roger's Park home on north shore of Lake Michigan in 1912. The Martin D'Arcy Museum of Art is housed within the Cudahy Library, which holds the bulk of Loyola's 1.3 million volumes, rare-book collections, and university archives. With a mission to educate the students, faculty, and staff of the university, it is the only museum in Chicago that focuses on medieval, Renaissance, and Baroque art and is open to the public. A permanent collection of over 500 works of art include exhibits of paintings by Bassano, Tintoretto, Guercino, and Stomer; Italian, German, and Flemish sculpture; French and Italian furniture and jewelry; and architectural elements from the focus periods. Liturgical vessels and processional crosses are also on display.

Highlights:
A rare Italian birth tray, depicting the legend of David and Goliath. During the Renaissance, the trays traditionally held gifts presented to new mothers at birth.

Mexican Fine Arts Center Museum

1852 West 19th Street
312-738-1503
www.mfacmchicago.org

Open: Tu–Su, 10:00 AM–5:00 PM
Admission: Free

The largest Mexican cultural institution in the country, the
Mexican Fine Arts Center Museum opened in 1987 in the heart
of Pilsen, the fastest growing Latino neighborhood in the city
and home to many colorful public murals that combine pre-
Columbian motifs with contemporary Latino concerns. Over
3500 objects in the museum's permanent collection include painting, sculpture, prints, drawings, photographs, and ephemera by
Mexican artists. An array of colonial and pre-Cuauhtemoc artifacts, textiles, devotional paintings, and carved saints are also part
of that collection. The ongoing exhibition, "Mexicanidad: Our
Past is Present," chronologically follows the history of Mexican
culture, its changes, struggles, and triumphs starting with
Colonial Mexico through the Revolution to present day Mexico
and the Mexican experience in the United States. The Visual
Arts Department presents changing exhibitions of ancient to
avant-garde art from Mexico and Mexican American communities, drawing from the permanent collection as well as from other
museums in this country and in Mexico.

Highlights:
Prints and drawings by Diego Rivera
Vintage posters of the United Farm Workers Union

Millennium Park

Michigan Avenue at Monroe Street

312-742-1168

www.millenniumpark.org

Open: Daily, dawn to dusk

Admission: Free

Unlike the great Chicago parks designed by nineteenth-century
landscape architects Frederick Law Olmsted and Daniel
Burnham, Millennium Park is a new kind of interactive urban
park. Downtown, across the street from the Art Institute of
Chicago, the 24-acre park is an outdoor center for art, music,
architecture and landscape design. Its centerpiece is the Jay
Pritzger Concert Pavilion, a sculptural band shell formed of
enormous flowing ribbons of steel with a trellis stretching over
the lawn and a snaking pedestrian bridge to Grant Park, designed
by Frank Gehry. With two 50-foot-tall glass block towers as
screens at each end of a reflecting pool, *Crown Fountain*, designed
by Spanish sculptor Jaume Plensa, projects giant changing faces
that periodically spew real streams of water into the pool. *Cloud
Gate*, a monumental 110-ton elliptical sculpture by British artist
Anish Kapoor, is forged of highly polished steel and sharply
reflects surrounding buildings, the park, and all passersby. The
Lurie Garden is enclosed by a *Broad Shoulder* hedge and is a
symbolic assemblage of plantings and light. The park also contains an indoor music and dance theater and the city's first indoor
bicycle parking facility, equipped with lockers, showers, a snack
bar, and bike rental and repair facilities

Mitchell Museum of the American Indian

2600 Central Park Avenue, Evanston
847-475-1030
www.mitchellmuseum.org

Open: Tu–Sa, 10:00 AM–5:00 PM; Th, 10:00 AM–8:00 PM; Su,
Noon–4:00 PM
Admission: Adults, $5; Seniors, Students, and Children, $2.50; Family
maximum, $10

Just north of Chicago in suburban Evanston, the Mitchell
Museum of Kendall College houses a permanent collection of
Native American artifacts dating from the Paleo-Indian period
through the present. Founded in 1977 with the collection of John
and Betty Mitchell, the collection has grown to more than 9,000
objects. Permanent exhibits are dedicated to Native cultures of
the Woodlands, Plains, Southwest, Northwest Coast, and
Arctic regions of North America. Collection strengths include
Great Lakes ice-fishing decoys, late nineteenth- and early twentieth-century Kachina dolls, and beadwork from the Northern
Plains and Great Lakes regions. Also included are Navajo weav-
ings, and arctic stone, ivory, and bone carvings dating from pre-
historic through modern times. Visitors can handle examples of
real artifacts and samples of raw materials used by Native
Americans, such as snake skin, birch bark, and caribou fur at
touching tables in each gallery. Over 5,000 books, periodicals,
and audio and videotapes are available in the library.

Highlights:
A full-size birch bark canoe in the Woodlands gallery

Museum of Contemporary Art

220 E. Chicago Avenue
312-280-2660
www.mcachicago.org

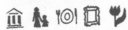

Open: W–Su, 10:00 AM–5:00 PM; Tu, 10:00 AM–8:00 PM
Admission: Adults, $10; Seniors and Students $6; Children 12 and
under, Free; Tuesday evenings, Free

Founded by a group of culturally concerned citizens recognizing
the need for an internationally known forum for contemporary
art in Chicago, the Museum of Contemporary Art opened in
1967. Starting out in a converted bakery, the MCA was the first
building in the United States to be wrapped by Christo. A new
aluminum and limestone-clad museum building referencing the
architecture of Mies van der Rohe was designed by Joseph Paul
Kleihues and opened in 1996. Located between Michigan
Avenue and Lake Michigan, the MCA is one of the largest
museums in the U.S. devoted to contemporary art, with 45,000
square feet of gallery space, a theater, a 15,000-volume art library,
and a permanent collection of more than 6,000 works of art created since 1945. Featured are minimalist, postminimalist, surreal-
ist, and conceptual works as well as video and artists books and a
34,000-square-foot outdoor sculpture garden. Focusing on temporary exhibitions and performances presenting groundbreaking
work by local, national, and international artists, exhibits include
installations of painting, sculpture, photography, video, film and
dance, and retrospectives of the work of some of today's most
important artists.

Highlights:

Cage by Magdalena Abakanowicz
Felt Suit by Joseph Bueys
Souvenir I, by Kerry James Marshall
Untitled, photographs by Cindy Sherman
Untitled, drawings by Raymond Pettibon
Letters and sculpture of H. C. Westermann

Museum of Contemporary Photography

600 S. Michigan Avenue
312-344-7104
www.mocp.org

Open: M–F, 10:00 AM–5:00 PM; Th, 10:00 AM–8:00 PM; Sa,
Noon–5:00 PM
Admission: Free

The only museum in the Midwest committed exclusively to the
medium of photography, the Museum of Contemporary
Photography is located in the south loop at Columbia College, a
progressive four-year private institution specializing in the arts
and media. Exhibitions explore photography's role as a medium
of communication and artistic expression, as a documenter of
life, as a vital tool used in science and technology, and as a commercial industry. Photographs produced in America since 1945
make up the permanent collection, and over 6,500 prints and
objects are periodically displayed and available for public viewing
by appointment. Rotating exhibitions showcase images by
nationally recognized artists and range in technique and theme
from photojournalism to scientific photography. The Midwest
Photographers Project introduces viewers to current work by
prominent and emerging regional artists. All works in the project
are loaned to the museum, rotated every two years, and available
for viewing in the Print Study Room. An archive houses the
artist's files, slides of other work, and biographical information.

Museum of Holography

1134 W. Washington Boulevard

312-226-1007

www.museumofholography.com

Open: W–Su, 12:30 PM–4:30 PM

Admission: Adults, $4; Children 6–12, $3; Children under 6, free

Holography developed with the invention of laser light in the early 1960s. Holograms are recordings of light waves reflected from an object illuminated with laser light, resulting in a three-dimensional image. The technology is applied in many ways ranging from medical imaging to the antifraud emblems on credit cards. The Museum of Holography is the only one of its kind in the United States, housing one of the world's largest collections of holograms and displaying the most popular. In a darkened gallery, exhibits include portraits and figures that appear to move or morph as visitors slowly pass by. Playful and eerie images are presented for viewer interaction in both large and small format: Michael Jordan maneuvers a basketball, a giant tarantula appears to make a move toward the viewer, and a miner pans for gold. Visitors experience X-ray vision as an almost life-size person is suddenly seen as a skeleton. Medical holograms with images of body organs and bones are the focus in an adjoining gallery, and the holographic process is explained in literature and by enthusiastic staff.

Highlights:

A hologram-in-the-round of Chicago newspaper columnist Mike Royko, who forms a smile as the image turns

A hologram of water appearing to pour out of a picture plane

Museum of Science and Industry

57th Street and Lake Shore Drive
773-684-1414
www.msichicago.org

Open: M–Sa, 9:30 AM–4:00 PM; Su, 11:00 AM–5:30 PM
Admission: Adults $9; Seniors $7.50; Children 3–11, $5

Incorporating the majestic Palace of Fine Arts, the only remaining building from the World's Columbian Exposition White City of 1893, the Museum of Science and Industry borders Lake Michigan in Frederick Law Olmsted–designed Jackson Park. Established in 1933 with funds donated by philanthropist and chairman of Sears, Roebuck, and Co., Julius Rosenwald, this hands-on museum now houses over 35,000 artifacts and 14 acres of interactive exhibits that inspire scientific inquiry and creativity. The largest science and industry museum in the western hemisphere, it houses a boardable submarine and jet plane, a 50-foot-deep simulation of a coal mine shaft that visitors can ride in, and a lunar module. The Henry Crown Space Center houses a five-story Omnimax Theater with a domed wraparound movie screen. At the museum's Imagination Station, young children can experiment with fundamental mechanics by building and floating boats in moving water and directing items with an electromagnetic crane. In the lobby, one of the world's largest continuously running model train dioramas traces the passenger and freight journey from Chicago to Seattle. In "Genetics: Decoding Life," visitors have the opportunity to learn about DNA and watch chicks emerge from eggs. "Imaging Tools of Science" illustrates the use of computer-based imaging technology in medicine, science, law enforcement, and entertainment. Visitors are invited to solve mysteries by applying the technology to forensics or to add their face to a database and see how computers color, mix, and contort facial features. Environmental science is featured in "Reusable City," where visitors can peer inside a landfill, trace water from its source to the tap, and monitor ozone.

Highlights:

U-505 German submarine captured by the U.S. Navy in World War II, which visitors can board. One of only five U-boats still in existence, it is the only one in the United States.

The Whispering gallery, constructed in 1937, invites visitors to whisper into one of two parabolic dishes and see how sound waves travel to a person at the other end of the room.

Toymaker 3000 consisting of interactive stations, moving robots, and a 2000-square-foot automated assembly line that can produce 300 toys per hour.

Naper Settlement

523 S. Webster Street, Naperville
630-420-6010
www.napersettlement.org

Open: Tu–Sa, 10:00 AM–4:00 PM; Su, 1:00 PM–4:00 PM (Apr–Oct);
Tu–F, 10:00 AM–4:00 PM (Nov–Mar)
Admission: Adults, $7; Seniors, $6; Children 4–17, $4.50 (summer);
Adults, $4.25; Seniors, $3.75; Children, $3 (winter)

A 13-acre living history museum located in downtown
Naperville, 30 miles west of Chicago, Naper Settlement tells the
story of how life changed for people in Northern Illinois towns
in the nineteenth century. From 1831 to 1900, Naperville grew
from a frontier outpost to a thriving turn-of-the-century community. In 1969 the Naperville Heritage Society began the
process of establishing the settlement by raising funds to save the
community's 1864 Gothic revival church. The church was moved
to property surrounding the Victorian-era Martin Mitchell
Mansion, built in 1883 and donated to the city of Naperville in
1936 by Caroline Martin Mitchell for the purpose of creating a
museum. Since then, a total of 30 historic buildings have been
relocated, recreated, or restored on the 13-acre site, including a
replica of the Pre-Emption House, the first hotel west of
Chicago, which also served as Naperville's county courthouse.
The settlement's main buildings include a typical 1830s log
house, fort, and one-room Copenhagen schoolhouse. A fire-
house stores Naperville's first 1874 hand-pumping fire engine.
The 1833 Paw Paw Post Office, and Daniels, Murray, and
Naper-Haight Houses are also available for viewing. A black-
smith shop and printing shop are operational. The settlement

houses 20,000 historical artifacts and a reference library. The buildings and homes are open for tours during the summer season when costumed interpreters bring history to life with educational activities in which visitors can participate. During the winter season the building interiors are closed, but visitors are invited to take a self-guided audio tour of the grounds. The visitor center remains open year round and offers special exhibits and the interactive exhibit "Brushstrokes of the Past . . . Naperville's Story."

Highlights

The newly-restored and lavishly furnished Martin Mitchell mansion reflects the lifestyle of one of Naperville's late nineteenth-century entrepreneurial families.

Nathan Manilow Sculpture Park

Governor's State University
University Parkway, University Park
708-534-5000
www.govst.edu

Open: M–F, 8:00 AM–10:30 PM; Sa, –6:00 PM; Su, 1:00 PM–9:00 PM;
Closed holidays
Admission: Free

Governor's State University was founded in 1969 as an experi-
mental college embodying the optimistic vision of the 1960s. In
1976 a new prairie campus, 40 minutes west of Chicago, was
built on 750 acres of natural and preserved landscape. The
Nathan Manilow Sculpture Park was established through the
combined efforts of Lewis Manilow, a well-known Chicago
patron of the arts, founding university president William E.
Engbretson, and world-renowned sculptor Mark Di Suvero.
Named in memory of Lewis Manilow's father, a land developer
and homebuilder in the far south suburbs, the park's first exhibit
of outdoor sculpture was called "The Sculptor, The Campus,
and The Prairie." Made mostly of scrap iron and steel, the
sculptures appeared in sharp contrast to their spacious pastoral
surroundings. By removing the art from a museum setting, it
took on new dimensions as viewers experienced it as part of the
landscape. The park's collection includes 22 monumental and
environmental works from the 1970s, 1980s, and 1990s by regional and internationally recognized sculptors. Open year-round
while classes are in session, visitors are invited to walk around
and enjoy the sculptures from many different angles and dis-
tances.

Highlights:

Mark Di Suvero's 1969 *For Lady Day*, a massive sculpture made of sections of a tank car suspended by cables and fastened to an assembly of welded steel girders

James Brenner's 1999 *Passage*, a steel maze made of 10-foot-tall interlocking half circles that form an interior visitors can enter

National Italian American Sports Hall of Fame

1431 Taylor Street
312-226-5566
www.niashf.org

Open: M–F, 9:00 AM–5:00 PM
Admission: $5

Riding on the success of the Italian American Boxing Hall of Fame, founded in 1977 by George Randazzo, the National Italian American Sports Hall of Fame was founded a year later. Dedicated to preserving and promoting the history and heritage of Italian Americans in sports, the Hall of Fame has enshrined over 200 athletes in annual induction ceremonies. With original headquarters in Elmwood Park and Arlington Heights, a new Hall of Fame opened in Chicago's "Little Italy" on the near west side in 2004. The Tommy and Jo Lasorda exhibit gallery features a five-screen, 25-foot multimedia display of video and sound. Sports memorabilia collected over 27 years is displayed in first-floor galleries and includes the winning race cars of Mario and Vince Andretti, Rocky Marciano's first heavyweight championship belt, and Vince Lombardi's last coat worn as coach of the Green Bay Packers. Call ahead to check on closings for special events.

National Viet Nam Veterans Art Museum

1801 S. Indiana Avenue

312-326-0270

www.nvvam.org

Open: M, 11:00 AM–5:00 PM; Tu–F, –6:00 PM; Sa, 10:00 AM–5:00 PM; Su, Noon–5:00 PM

Admission: Adults, $6; Seniors and Students, $5; Mondays,$1; Memorial Day and Veteran's Day, Free

Brought together by a commitment to tell the story of the Vietnam War through the artwork of the men and women who served in that conflict, the Viet Nam Veterans Arts Group was formed in the 1970s. With a mission to encourage a better understanding of the personal consequences of war, the National Viet Nam Veterans Art Museum opened in a former warehouse in the Prairie Avenue historical district in 1996. A fine-art collection of over 1,000 pieces includes drawings made with C-rations and coffee. It includes works by artist-veterans who served in all branches of the military as well as the militaries of Australia, Cambodia, Thailand, and North and South Viet Nam. Former prisoners of war are among the exhibited artists. Three floors of highly emotional, graphic, and often violent experiences are recollected and expressed through paintings, drawings, photography, sculpture, collage, poetry, and prose. Subjects range from the moving imagery of a mother receiving news of her son's death in the painting *We Regret to Inform You*, by Cleveland Wright, to an assemblage of teak and 50-caliber shell casings in *Dressed to Kill* by Joseph C. Fornelli.

Featured is a photographic journal of a soldier's life among the Vietnamese, narrated in poetry by the photographer.

Highlights:

"Above and Beyond Memorial Sculpture," a permanent assemblage of over 58,000 dog tags suspended in a wind chime configuration from a 24-foot-high atrium ceiling. Each tag is imprinted with a name for every American killed in the Viet Nam War.

Newberry Library

60 W. Walton Street
312-943-9090
www.newberry.org

Open: M, F, Sa, 8:15 AM–5:30 PM; Tu, W, Th, 8:15 AM–7:30 PM
(Gallery); F, Sa, 9:00 AM–5:00 PM; Tu, W, Th, 10:00 AM–6:00 PM
(Reading Hours)
Admission: Free

In the 1850s, Chicago pioneer of commerce William Loomis
Newberry willed that his estate fund a free public library. With
the founding of the Chicago Public Library in 1876, the trustees
of the estate were free to establish the Newberry Library as a
reference library of unique collections. In 1893 the city's three
major libraries—the Chicago Public, the Newberry, and the
Crerar—agreed to specialize and divide their collections, with
the Newberry focusing on history and the humanities. The current home of the Newberry was designed by its first librarian,
William Frederick Poole, and architect Henry Ives Cobb and
constructed that year. The Newberry's collection numbers 1.5
million books, 5 million manuscript pages, and 300,000 historic
maps. One of the leading independent research institutions of
the world, the collection includes history and literature of
Western European civilizations from the Middle Ages through
World War I, and of the Americas from the first contact
between Europeans and Native Americans. It also contains rich
resources for twentieth-century Chicago history, genealogy, car-
tography, and printing. Two exhibit galleries are open to the public providing venues for traveling exhibitions of artifacts, manuscripts, maps, prints, and documents that interpret the library's

research and collections, which are supported by Newberry objects. A series of small displays called "Yours To Explore" highlight the collections on a rotating basis and demonstrate that through the humanities connections are made between the past and the present and with lives of people in the western world. The library is open to all readers 16 and over with a library card.

Highlights:

Illustrated manuscripts and woodcuts from the fifteenth to nineteenth centuries

"Plan of Chicago" theoretical reconstruction illustrations by Daniel H. Burnham and Edward H. Bennett from 1909

Oriental Institute Museum

1155 East 58th Street
773-702-9514
www.oi.uchicago.edu

Open: Tu–Sa, 10:00 AM–6:00 PM; W, –8:30 PM; Su, Noon–6:00 PM;
Closed Mondays
Admission: Free

Located on the Hyde Park campus, the University of Chicago's Oriental Institute Museum exhibits one of the world's major collections of antiquities from Egypt, Iran, Syria, Palestine, and Anatolia. Conducting research and archaeological expeditions to the Near East since 1919, the museum houses one of the largest collections of Mesopotamian objects outside of Iraq. With individual galleries dedicated to regions, three millennia of art and artifacts are displayed ranging from monolithic figures to intricately carved stone seals.

Exhibits trace the development of writing with examples of hieroglyphics and cuneiform dealing with literature, mathematics, and science and include clay and stone tablets and papyrus scrolls. Sculptures and relief carvings depict people and objects used in ancient Egyptian daily life. A 17-foot-tall statue of King Tutankhamman dominates the Egyptian gallery, and an exhibit discussing funerary beliefs includes a Roman-era mummy of a five-year-old boy. Plates from royal tables of Persepolis that were broken when Alexander the Great destroyed the city in 331 BC are displayed in the Persian gallery, and examples of the world's first coinage are also on view. The Mesopotamia gallery contains an interactive touch screen for children.

Highlights:

A 16-foot-tall human-headed winged bull from Korsabad, flanked by tall stone reliefs that stood with it in the palace of Assyrian king Sargon II, ruler from 721-705 BC

A colossal head of a bull made of polished black limestone that once guarded the entrance to Hundred-Column Hall of Persepolis from 520 to 331 B.C.

Peggy Notebaert Nature Museum

2430 N. Cannon Drive
773-755-5100
www.chias.org

Open: M–F, 9:00 AM–4:30 PM; Sa & Su, 10:00 AM–5:00 PM
Admission: Adults, $7; Seniors and Students $5; Children 3–12, $4;
Thursdays, Free

The Chicago Academy of Sciences became Chicago's first museum in 1857 when the Midwestern prairie had already begun to disappear beneath an increasing number of farms and towns. A young naturalist, Robert Kennicott, and a group of others concerned about the disappearance of native plants and animals founded the academy as a home for their scientific papers and collections. In 1999 the museum expanded to become the Peggy Notebaert Nature Museum, located in Lincoln Park. Conveying the importance of environmental stewardship, the museum is surrounded by native trees, plants, and wildlife. Grounds containing gardens representing five regional ecosystems include a wetlands pond where visitors are invited to sit and enjoy the sights and sounds of nature.

Permanent exhibits examine the relationship between people and nature and explore the ways humans impact their environment. Visitors learn through interactive exhibits how even city dwellers are connected to the environment and the steps they can take to help "nurture nature." Children under 7 can explore habitats and climb a two-story tree house to discover how trees grow and all the creatures that live in them. Snakes, tadpoles, praying mantids, and other animals are collected, bred, and raised by museum scientists learning how to ensure the survival of endangered species. Visitors can observe their care and maintenance in the Look-in Animal Lab. A 28-foot-tall greenhouse with a blooming garden filled with live butterflies from seven countries around the world encourages visitors of all ages to walk through and enjoy contact with one of nature's most beautiful creatures. Interactive graphics detail their lifecycles, migration, and behavior, and the museum is home to the only butterfly-breeding lab of its kind in North America

Highlights:
Native butterflies emerging from their chrysalises
A blue-winged Common Morpho butterfly in flight

Pleasant Home

217 Home Avenue, Oak Park
708-383-2654
www.pleasanthome.org

Open: Th–Su, 12:30 PM, 1:30 PM, 2:30 PM (Guided Tours)
Admission: Adults, $5; Seniors and Students, $3; Children under 5, Free;
Thursdays, Free

A 30-room mansion designed by prominent Prairie School
architect George W. Maher, Pleasant Home was built in 1897
for John Farner, investment banker and philanthropist. Located
in the Oak Park historic district, the seven-acre property, now
known as Mills Park, was sold to the park district by the house's
second owners, the Mills family. Maher, who developed a style
distinctive from Frank Lloyd Wright and other Prairie School
architects, was known for a "motif-rhythm" theory in design,
which was developed in Pleasant Home, one of the earliest and
most distinguished examples of the Prairie School of architecture. The house's simple horizontal exterior is enhanced by
Roman brick cladding, a low-pitched roof, broad entrance porch,
and unadorned elements. Interior features include expansive windows, intricate woodwork, art glass, and custom furniture and
light fixtures, all of which incorporate repeated decorative motifs.

Highlights:

Art glass, especially the window over the stairwell in the front
entrance hall

Dining room table and chairs designed by Maher

Polish Museum of America

984 N. Milwaukee Avenue
773-384-3352
www.pma.prcua.org

Open: M–Su, 11:00 AM–4:00 PM. Closed Thursdays
Admission: Adults, $3; Students and Seniors, $2; Children under 12, $1

The oldest and largest ethnic museum in the country, the Polish Museum of America was founded in 1937 and located in Chicago's first Polish settlement neighborhood. With the largest wave of Polish immigration taking place between the Civil War and World War I, Chicago's population of Poles grew into the largest outside of Warsaw. The 1939 World's Fair in New York included a large exhibition of Polish art and artifacts sponsored by the Polish government. But when the invasion of Poland set off World War II, they could not be returned, and Chicago's Polish community purchased 75 percent of the collection of paintings, sculpture, ornaments, folk art, and artifacts. Today these items make up two-thirds of the museum's permanent collection. Also exhibited are traditional folk and military costumes and tributes to famous Poles, including nineteenth-century Shakespearean actress Helena Modrzejewska and Pope John Paul II. An art gallery contains nineteenth and twentieth century paintings of events in Polish history, Social Realist portraits, city and landscapes, bronze and stone portrait busts, and figurines from the Cmielow porcelain factory. The museum archives preserves documents pertaining to Polish and Polish American history, and a library contains over 60,000 volumes, 250 periodicals, and recordings of Polish music.

Highlights:

A winged suit of Husaria armor (Polish Infantry)

Rare Polish texts from the sixteenth to eighteenth centuries

A monumental painting of Polish American Civil War hero —
Pulaski at Savannah by Stanislaw Batowski

A bas-relief carved in salt from the mine at Wieliczka

Pullman Visitor Center

11141 S. Cottage Grove Avenue
773-785-8901
www.pullmanil.org

Open: Tu–Su, 11:00 AM–3:00 PM
Admission: Adults, $3; Seniors and Students, $2

Industrialist George M. Pullman achieved fame and success in 1865 when *Pioneer*, the luxurious sleeping rail car he prototyped and designed, was linked to Abraham Lincoln's funeral train. In 1867 he founded Pullman's Palace Car Company and by the 1870s had factories in four cities, which manufactured sleeping, dining, parlor, and drawing-room cars. The company maintained ownership of these cars, leasing them to railroads, fully staffed, to provide top-quality service for the guests. In 1879 Pullman purchased 4,000 acres of land 14 miles south of downtown Chicago. Here he built a Pullman car factory complex and a model town for its workers. The town became famous throughout the world for its affordable housing and amenities, which included indoor plumbing, parks, churches, schools, and a health-care system. His objective was to strengthen his business by recognizing that working people "are the most important element which enters into the successful operation of any manufacturing enterprise." Indeed, the town's reputation attracted talented craftsmen from around the country. By 1890 there were more than 1,700 working residents inhabiting block after block of signature red brick row houses and flats. But a major depression in 1893 led to a serious decline in business, and when forced to cut wages, Pullman refused to negotiate with workers. Thousands were laid off, and Railway Union members responded with a strike that led to a national boycott of trains pulling Pullman cars. The business survived for many years, but the model city had a tarnished reputation. Today, portions of the original Pullman district are intact, while others are undergoing restoration. Visitors should keep in mind that the town is not a museum, but an active residential community. The visitor's center documents the dramatic era with a small display of Pullman car artifacts, photographs, newspaper clippings, and neighborhood tours.

Highlights

The once grand Hotel Florence, in operation from 1881–1975. It offered patrons the only bar allowed in Pullman before 1900. Greenstone Church which Pullman hoped would be used for all denominations.

Regenstein Library, Special Collections Gallery, the University of Chicago

1100 East 57th Street
773-702-8705
www.lib.uchicago.edu/spcl/exhpub.html

Open: M–F, 8:30 AM–4:45 PM
Admission: Free; visitors must register at front desk to enter

The prestigious University of Chicago boasts 78 Nobel Prize winners associated with the university as faculty, students, or researchers. The south side institution is a national leader in higher education and research. Founded in 1890, the university library's holdings include a rare-book collection of over 265,000 volumes and manuscripts ranging from medieval and Renaissance materials to records on atomic scientist organizations to the editorial files of "Poetry: A Magazine of Verse." The Regenstein Library, designed by Walter Netsch in 1970, is the largest building on campus, almost one block square, and it houses materials in the humanities and social sciences and the Special Collections Research Center. The center offers four to five scholarly exhibits a year drawn from the university's holdings as well as from other sources. The main exhibition gallery features in-depth exhibitions on subjects ranging from the history of public health to book use and theory to contemporary poetry. The Ludwig Rosenberger Library of Judaica Gallery, located within in the center, exhibits rare materials examining the history and sources of Jewish thought, and the Alcoves gallery displays rare books and documents by theme. The general public is invited to view the exhibitions but must apply for a day pass at the library's entrance.

Robie House

5757 S. Woodlawn Avenue
773-834-1847
www.wrightplus.org/new

Open: M–F, 11:00 AM, 1:00 PM, 3:00 PM (Guided Tours); Sa & Su,
11:00 AM–3:30 PM (Guided Tours every 20 minutes)
Admission: Adults, $9; Seniors and Children 7–18, $7

Considered one of the most important buildings in the history of
American architecture, the Robie House, designed by Frank
Lloyd Wright, represents the culmination of Prairie Style, incorporating ideas of nature and landscape with natural materials and
open, integrated interior spaces. With cantilevered roofs that
extend 20 feet beyond the walls at each end of the house, 174 art
glass windows, and doors that open the floor plan and transform
outer walls, the house remains a masterpiece of innovative architectural form. Built in 1910 for Frederick C. Robie, the house has
been used as a private residence for three families, a dormitory,
and office space for three different institutions. Twice threatened
with demolition, ownership of the house was transferred from
the University of Chicago to the Frank Lloyd Wright
Preservation Trust in 1997, when it began to implement badly
needed restoration. Located on the University of Chicago campus, the Robie House is paid tribute in the dynamic design of
the Graduate School of Business building on an adjacent lot.
Some of the original furniture designed by Wright for the house
is on display in the Modern Art and Design collection of the
Smart Museum of Art, also on campus. Guided tours explain
the architectural significance of the house, and are available
throughout the current restoration. Junior tours are also available.

Second Presbyterian Church

1936 S. Michigan Avenue
312-225-4951

Open: Tu–F, 9:00 AM–5:00 PM; Call ahead for an appointment
Admission: Free

When this neo-Gothic Church was designed by New York
architect James Renwick, the neighborhood, which included
Prairie Avenue, was home to families of the most affluent indus-
trialists and businessmen in Chicago. The elegant interior decorations reflect the congregation that built the church in 1874 and
then rebuilt it after a fire in 1900. The restoration, designed by
architect and member Howard Van Doren Shaw and muralist
Frederick Clay Bartlett, dramatically transformed the sanctuary
into the English Arts and Crafts style. New decorations included
Tiffany stained-glass windows, atmospheric murals depicting pro-
cessions of angels with musical instruments in a starry sky, and
geometric designs in relief on the ceiling with Gothic-grotesque
animals at intersections. There are over 175 representations of
angels, including four heralding angels high above the front of the
sanctuary and carved angels supporting chandeliers. The interior
is lined with dark oak beams and trim and lit by candelabra and
chandeliers designed by Shaw. Over the years the neighborhood
became industrialized and fell into disrepair, but with the restoration of historic Prairie Avenue, the church's interior elements are
recognized as rare and fragile treasures. Religious services and
events are held regularly, and visitors are asked to be respectful
and to call for appointments for viewing.

Smart Museum of Art

5550 S. Greenwood Avenue
773-702-0200
www.smartmuseum.uchicago.edu

Open: Tu, W, F, 10:00 AM–4:00 PM; Th, –8:00 PM; Sa & Su, 11:00
AM–5:00 PM (regular hours); Tu–F, 10:00 AM–4:00 PM; Sa & Su, 11:00
AM–4:00 PM (summer hours)
Admission: Free

With a permanent of collection of 7,500 works of art spanning
five centuries of Western and Eastern civilizations, the David
and Alfred Smart Museum of Art is located on the University
of Chicago campus. Established in 1974 by David Smart, the
Chicago-based founder of *Esquire* magazine, and his brother
Alfred, the museum's original purpose was to house a variety of
art objects previously used for study in academic departments,
including Greek and Roman antiquities, and objects used in
Chinese studies and the field of comparative religion. Established
as a separate entity in 1983, the collection was expanded and public outreach programs instituted. Objects are displayed in galleries
devoted to Old Master paintings, sculpture, and decorative arts;
arts of Asia, and modern art and design featuring works created
from the 1880s to the 1950s. Galleries also feature contemporary
art with a focus on figurative works and works on paper including
drawings, prints, calligraphy, and photographs. A sculpture garden contains work by contemporary American and European
artists. Special exhibitions are regularly mounted, and collections
are rotated to allow audiences to view works in new contexts.

Highlights:
Furniture designed by Frank Lloyd Wright for the Robie House

Smith Museum of Stained Glass Windows

600 E. Grand Avenue on Navy Pier
312-595-5024

Open: Su–Th, 10:00 AM–8:00 PM; F–Sa, –10:00 PM
Admission: Free

Located on Lake Michigan near the mouth of the Chicago River, Navy Pier was built in 1916 as part of the Burnham Plan for a recreational pier and to meet the city's need for a modern harbor facility. It was renovated as a 50-acre shopping and recreational facility in 1989. The Smith Museum of Stained Glass Windows occupies an 800-foot-expanse on the lower level terraces of Festival Hall. The first of its kind in the country, the collection includes 150 colorful stained-glass windows displayed with back lighting. Works by Frank Lloyd Wright, Louis Sullivan, John LaFarge, and Louis Comfort Tiffany are featured; and the collection is divided into four themes: Victorian religious windows, Victorian secular windows, designs of the Prairie School, and contemporary designs. Most of the decorative windows come from Chicago churches, public buildings, and private homes and were made between 1870 and the present. National and ethnic styles of Chicago's European immigrants are reflected in the religious windows, and the history of architecture and decorative art in the secular ones. Contemporary works include windows by Chicago artists Ed Pashke and Roger Brown, a portrait of Dr. Martin Luther King, and a window made of pop bottles.

Spertus Museum of Judaica

618 S. Michigan Avenue
312-322-1747
www.spertus.edu

Open: Su–W, 10:00 AM–5:00 PM; Th, –7:00 PM; F, –3:00 PM;
Rosenbaum ARTiFACT Center: Su–Th, 1:00 PM–4:30 PM; F, –3:00 PM
Admission: Adults, $5; Seniors, Students, and Children, $3

The largest Jewish Museum between the two coasts, Spertus
Museum is located on the first floor of the Spertus Institute for
Jewish Studies on south Michigan Avenue, across the street
from Grant Park. Spanning 3,500 years of Jewish history from
antiquity to the present day, the museum houses a permanent
collection of over 10,000 artifacts and works of art from
Western, Central, and Eastern Europe; North Africa; the
Middle East; and United States. While most of the permanent
collection is no longer displayed, it includes a rich array of Jewish
ceremonial art from the seventeenth century to present and
archaeological artifacts dating from the Bronze Age through
Byzantine period, including oil lamps, vessels, coins, ceramic toys,
funerary objects, and cosmetic items. A fine-art collection
includes paintings, graphics, and sculptures by nineteenth- and
twentieth-century American, Israeli, and European artists, and
temporary exhibitions exploring Jewish history, culture, and religion are emphasized. Children are invited to discover clues about
life in ancient times by unearthing artifacts on a model tel, (an
archaeological dig site) in the Rosenbaum ARTiFACT Center.
The Israelite House contains props, puppets, and a baking oven
for preschoolers to pretend in, and older children can learn about
ancient musical instruments and play the Travel and Trade game.

Highlights:

Bezalel Torah Ark made of brass, semiprecious stones, enamel, silver, ivory, and shell

A collection of paintings and prints by artist Todros Geller

State of Illinois Art Collection

James R. Thompson Center
100 W. Randolph Street
www.state.il.us

🏛 🍽 🖼

Open: M–F, 8:30 AM–5:00 PM
Admission: Free; Must present photo ID at each floor

The largest single collection of contemporary Illinois artwork is located in the State of Illinois James R. Thompson Center. The center—a blue, salmon, and gray glass-enclosed steel structure designed by Helmut Jahn—houses state offices, shopping facilities, and more than 150 works of art by Illinois artists. Works were purchased through the Percent for Art Program established in 1977, which appropriates one-half of one percent of the construction cost of state-funded buildings to be used for the purchase of art. Paintings, sculpture, and ceramics are available for viewing in the public areas of the building, just steps away from the elevators on the third through ninth floors. Visitors must present a photo ID to the guard stationed on each floor before accessing the artwork, since it is installed adjacent to offices and employee facilities. On the second floor, the Illinois State Museum Chicago gallery exhibits artwork and crafts by local artists.

Highlights:
American Buffalo, a painting by Roger Brown on the fourth floor
Yellow Oracle, a painting by Vera Klement, on the ninth floor

Swedish American Museum

5211 N. Clark Street
773-728-8111
www.samac.org

Open: Tu–F, 10:00 AM–4:00 PM; Sa & Su, 11:00 AM–4:00 PM
(Children's Museum opens at 1:00 PM on weekdays)
Admission: Adults, $4; Seniors, Students, and Children 3 and over, $3

Over one million Swedes immigrated to the United States from
1845 to 1930, drawn to available farmland and the labor market in
cities like Chicago. The Swedish colony in Chicago grew to be
the largest in the United States, and by 1920 Swedes dominated
several north-side neighborhoods, including Andersonville, home
to the Swedish American Museum. Opening in 1976, with several expansions since, the three- story storefront museum houses
the permanent exhibit "A Dream of America, An Immigrant's
Journey," which includes a reproduced Swedish American parlor
in 1920s Chicago; a room dedicated to Raoul Wallenberg, the
Swedish statesman who courageously saved Jews from Nazi
death camps; a collection of Swedish art, folk costumes, music,
and an introduction to the Swedish language. Temporary exhibits
on Swedish themes are also presented. The third floor Children's
Museum of Immigration is an interactive, hands-on museum for
children ages 3–12. Children can board a 20-foot steamship to
America to start a new life in a furnished pioneer's log cabin. A
replica Viking ship is available for exploration, and a refugee's raft
tells a story of today's immigration. While the museum has a
Swedish focus, the story of Swedish immigration parallels that of
many other groups who left the old world behind to find new
lives in America.

Highlights:

An authentic reproduction of a century-old Swedish farmhouse, or stuga, where children can don 1850s-style costumes and milk a cow, collect eggs, or churn butter

Tribune Tower

435 N. Michigan Avenue
312- 222-3232

Open: Daily
Admission: Free

In 1922 Chicago *Tribune* publisher Colonel Robert McCormick
organized a design competition for a new skyscraper to house the
major daily newspaper operations. The Gothic-style winning
entry designed by New York's Raymond Hood and John
Howells went against the modernizing trend set by the Chicago
School, which reduced decorations to a minimum. The new
Tribune Tower was modeled after the Button Tower of the
Rouen Cathedral in France, with flying buttresses and a striking
silhouette. But before its completion in 1925, McCormick
ordered his foreign correspondents to collect and bring back fragments from famous sites from all over the world to be embedded
in the tower's exterior walls. The 136 embedded fragments are
labeled, and many are visible from the sidewalk, among them, are
stones from the Parthenon, Taj Mahal, Westminster Abbey, the
Great Wall of China, and the Alamo.

Ukrainian Institute of Modern Art

2320 Chicago Avenue
773-227-5522
www.uima.org

Open: W–Su, Noon–4:00 PM
Admission: Free

With an emphasis on abstract art, the Ukrainian Institute of
Modern Art was founded in 1971 as an alternate exhibit space in
three converted storefronts in Ukrainian Village. With a sleek,
updated façade by Chicago architect Stanley Tigerman, UIMA
houses the largest permanent collection of fine art by Ukrainian
American artists in the United States, including paintings,
abstract and figurative sculpture, drawings, woodcuts, litho-
graphs, and screen prints. The institute also dedicates a large
gallery to six rotating exhibits of contemporary art a year, two of
which are devoted to Ukrainian artists.

Highlights:
A serigraph by Alexander Archipenko

Ukranian National Museum of Chicago

2249 W. Superior Street
312-421-8020
www.ukrntlmuseum.com

Open: Th–Su, 11:00 AM–4:00 PM; M–W (by appointment)
Admission: Adults, $4; Children under 12, Free

The second largest country in Europe, Ukraine gained independence after the collapse of the Soviet Union in 1991. Located in historic Ukrainian Village, a neighborhood where businesses and churches with ethnic origins cater to a gentrifying population, the Ukrainian National Museum was founded in 1952. Over 1,000 artifacts are included in the museum collection, including folk costumes representing Ukraine's many regions and examples of traditional crafts such as embroidered textiles and beadwork. Tsymbaly, musical instruments known in the Ukraine since the sixteenth century, are displayed, as well as a fragment of a sixteenth-century Kozak burial shroud and centuries old books and weaponry. Permanent exhibits document the aftermath of the 1986 Chernobyl disaster with photographs, and memorialize the famine-genocide that occurred in the 1930s under Stalin's dictatorship. The museum houses a library of over 16,000 books, periodicals, and newspapers and an archive, including material about Ukrainian communities, particularly in Chicago.

Highlights:

A rich collection of Pysanky, which are intricately decorated eggs with geometric designs. The tradition predates Christianity, and design motifs signify protection and friendship.

Unity Temple

875 Lake Street, Oak Park
708-383-8873
www.unitytemple-utrf.org

Open: M–F, 10:30 AM–4:30 PM; Sa & Su, 1:00 PM–4:00 PM (Mar–Nov);
Daily, 1:00 PM–4:00 PM (Dec–Feb)
Admission: Adults, $7; Seniors and Children 6–22, $5; Children 5 and
under, Free

Considered to be one of the country's greatest architectural
achievements, Oak Park's Unity Temple was designed by Frank
Lloyd Wright and opened in 1908. It is his last surviving public
building and the one he claimed represented the birth of modern
architecture. Wright, a resident of Oak Park and member of the
Unitarian Universalist congregation, was commissioned to design
the building after lightening destroyed the original temple in 1905.
Using cast-in-place concrete as structural and decorative material, Wright created a dramatic façade and secluded interior serving
as both a place for worship and community gathering. The temple displays typical Prairie style features with cubical forms, 19
separate roof planes placed at different levels, and cantilevered
rooflines extending 5 feet beyond exterior walls. Receding planes
and wood trim define the interior by leading the eye from pulpit
to balconies, columns, and stairs. Skylights and art-glass windows, some featuring the tree-of-life, illuminate the space and are
complemented by geometric Wright-designed light fixtures.
Designated a national historic landmark in 1971, the Restoration
Foundation was formed in 1973 and plans to complete restoration
in 2008, the one hundredth anniversary of building.

Water Tower and Pumping Station

806 N. Michigan Avenue
(312) 742-0808
www.cityofchicago.org

Open: M–Sa, 10:00 AM–6:30 PM; Su, 10:00 AM–5:00 PM
Admission: Free

The Old Chicago Water Tower stands like a medieval castle on
Michigan Avenue in the heart of the Magnificent Mile. Built in
1869 out of limestone blocks, it was one of the few buildings to
survive the great Chicago fire in 1871 and served as a guidepost in
the aftermath as people searched through charred remains for
what was left of their homes. Though no longer operating, inside
is a 138-foot-tall standpipe once connected to an under water
tunnel that extended two miles out into Lake Michigan for a
source of cleaner water. Across the street is the original pumping
station, built of the same stone and still pumping about 250 million gallons of water a day. Inside, tremendous pumps and their
pipes can be viewed from behind a glass barrier. The water tower
also houses the City gallery, showing changing exhibits by
Chicago photographers, and the pumping station contains a
tourist information office with restrooms, a café, and a theater.

Willie Dixon's Blues Heaven

2120 S. Michigan Avenue
312-808-1286
www.bluesheaven.com

Open: Tours by appointment only
Admission: $10

Chess Records, founded by brothers Leonard and Phil Chess, is internationally known as the site of some the greatest blues recordings between 1957 and 1967. This Michigan Avenue location was the creative home of such artists as Muddy Waters, Howlin' Wolf, Sonny Boy Williamson, Koko Taylor, and Chuck Berry. Willie Dixon, who wrote over 500 blues compositions, was employed by Chess as an accompanist and studio manager and was friend and mentor to countless blues and rock and roll artists, including the Rolling Stones. After Chess's collapse, Willie Dixon organized the Blues Heaven Foundation in 1982 to promote awareness about the blues and help musicians regain royalty rights. At the time of his death in 1992, the old Chess Records building was slated for demolition; and at her husband's request, Marie Dixon purchased the building as a home for the foundation. Opened to the public in 1997 for guided tours and workshops, the recording rooms remain with several pieces of equipment similar to what was used there in the past. The tour guide's account of the lively years at Chess records is complemented by display cases containing memorabilia and personal effects of some of the artists, such as the boots, hat, vest, and fringed leather jacket of the King of Maxwell Street Blues, Jimmy Lee Roberts; the signature hat and suit of

Willie Dixon with his hand-written song lyrics; and sequined performing gown and shoes of Koko Taylor.

Highlights:

A wall of 38 plaster life masks of Blues performers, cast between 2002 and 2004, with a short biography for each, including such greats as Bo Diddley, Blind Mississippi Morris, Odetta, Pinetop Perkins, Charlie Musselwaite, and Koko Taylor

Appendix

The following lists are thematic guides to the collections of the museums in Chicago. All lists are in alphabetical order

TEN MUSEUMS FOR CHILDREN
Adler Planetarium and Astronomy Museum
Bronzeville Children's Museum
Chicago Children's Museum
Field Museum of Natural History
Health World
Millennium Park
Museum of Science and Industry
Naper Settlement
Peggy Notebaert Nature Museum
Spertus Museum of Judaica

TEN MUSEUMS FOR TEENAGERS
Adler Planetarium and Astronomy Museum
Art Institute of Chicago
Cantigny Park
Field Museum of Natural History
International Museum of Surgical Science
Millennium Park
Museum of Holography
Museum of Science and Industry
Naper Settlement
Oriental Institute Museum

TEN MUSEUMS — AMERICAN HISTORY
A. Philip Randolph Pullman Porter Museum
Cantigny Park
Charles Gates Dawes House Museum
Chicago Historical Society
Clarke House Museum
DuSable Museum of African-American History
Frank Lloyd Wright Home and Studio
Jane Addams Hull-House Museum
Mitchell Museum of the American Indian
Naper Settlement

TEN MUSEUMS — ART & ARCHITECTURE
Art Institute of Chicago
Block Museum of Art
Martin D'Arcy Museum of Art
Mexican Fine Arts Center Museum
Museum of Contemporary Art
Museum of Contemporary Photography
Nathan Manilow Sculpture Park
National Viet Nam Veterans Art Museum
Smart Museum of Art
Smith Museum of Stained Glass Windows

Ten Museums—Regional Interest
A. Philip Randolph Pullman Porter Museum
Chicago Historical Society
D. L. Moody Museum
Frank Lloyd Wright Home and Studio
Harold Washington Library Center
Labor History Museum
Naper Settlement
Pullman Visitor Center
Water Tower and Pumping Station
Willie Dixon's Blues Heaven

Ten Museums—Science and Technology
Adler Planetarium and Astronomy Museum
Field Museum of Natural History
Health World
International Museum of Surgical Science
Lizzadro Museum of Lapidary Arts
Museum of Science and Industry
Museum of Holography
Peggy Notebaert Nature Museum
Regenstein Library
Water Tower and Pumping Station

CULTURAL MUSEUMS
Balzekas Museum of Lithuanian Culture
Chinese-American Museum of Chicago
DuSable Museum of African-American History
Hellenic Museum and Cultural Center
Irish American Heritage Center
Latvian Folk Art Museum
Mexican Fine Arts Center Museum
Polish Museum of America
Spertus Museum of Judaica
Swedish American Museum
Ukrainian National Museum

HISTORIC HOUSE MUSEUMS
Cantigny Park
Charles Gates Dawes House
Charnley-Persky House
Clarke House
Frank Lloyd Wright Home and Studio
Glessner House
Jane Addams Hull House Museum
Madlener House
Pleasant Home
Robie House

MUSEUMS THAT REQUIRE APPOINTMENTS
Irish American Heritage Center Museum
Labor History Museum
Second Presbyterian Church
Willie Dixon's Blues Heaven

Index of Alternative Museum Names